I0459432

SPORTS SKILLS FOR YOUNG ATHLETES

Master Mental Toughness, Resilience, Teamwork, Confidence, Motivation, Discipline, and So Much More!

JAMIE MYERS

ISBN: 978-1-957590-50-9

For questions, email: Support@AwesomeReads.org

Please consider writing a review!

Just visit: <u>AwesomeReads.org/review</u>

Copyright 2025. All Rights Reserved.

No part of this book may be reproduced or transmitted in any form or by any means, electronic or mechanical, including photocopying, recording, or by any other form without written permission from the publisher.

FREE BONUS

SCAN TO GET OUR NEXT BOOK FOR FREE!

TABLE OF CONTENTS

INTRODUCTION

Being a kid means that a lot of your life is about going to school and spending time on activities you enjoy. Many kids choose to participate in sports or other athletic activities like soccer, gymnastics, or baseball. These activities are great ways to improve your physical skills and mental well-being. They also allow you to connect with other kids and share your passions.

There's no doubt that athletics is one of the best parts of being a kid. Think of that moment at school when it's finally gym class. You get to leave your desk and move your body. You can run around and even be a little loud. You feel the fresh air on your face as you pump your feet and challenge yourself to run faster and play better.

You likely have tons of energy, and sports are a great way to focus that energy on something that has good results and can help you become a better person overall. Yes, these activities take a lot of work, but when you're willing to put in that work, you discover something well worth all that effort.

For some, sports are just a way to have fun, but lots of kids also want to compete. You may even want to focus on sports as a job when you grow up. Doing well in sports and athletics isn't an easy task for young people, but you can learn to have a champion mindset, which means that you start thinking like the top players in the game. With a champion mindset, you can get better at your sport and learn valuable lessons for a bright future.

If you're a kid who wants to improve your athletic skills and learn how to be a champion, you're in the right place. Just because you're a kid doesn't mean you can't do amazing things. It's time to start learning how to think like a champion. Whether you want to have a career as a sports star or you just want to do your best, it's time to act like a champion. You can do it!

[1]
UNDERSTANDING THE CHAMPION MINDSET

As a kid, you should be having a lot of fun, but that doesn't mean you don't have to take things seriously. If you're serious about athletics, you need to have a champion mindset. But what is a champion mindset, and how can you use it to be better at sports and other activities you love? You'll learn the answers to these questions right now.

WHAT IS A CHAMPION MINDSET?

To better understand a champion mindset, it helps to break it down into its individual words: *champion* and *mindset*.

Let's look at the word *champion* first. The most common definition of a champion is someone who wins first prize, but being a champion isn't just about winning all the time. A champion is willing to work hard and fight for what they want. Champions lose sometimes, but they know how to learn from their losses. When you are a champion, you keep trying, even when things aren't going your way.

Mindset means how you think. If you're playing a sport, and you're thinking, "I'm so bad at this," you likely have a negative mindset. A positive mindset would be thinking about how much you're learning or how much fun you're having while playing your sport.

You may not be able to help how you feel, but you can influence your mindset by taking actions that create useful habits or behaviors that you do over and over. As you create new habits, you will form a champion mindset.

Having a champion mindset means that you know that you can keep going even if your team always seems to lose. Instead of

4

focusing on your losses, you choose to work harder and keep practicing until you can lead your team to victory.

When you have a champion mindset, you know that you can achieve your dreams. You don't let negativity ruin your progress. You know that when things get hard, you shouldn't quit. You keep going because you are passionate and want to be the best you can be. You accept losses with grace and find ways to improve even when you win.

THE IMPORTANCE OF MENTAL TOUGHNESS

The focus of sports is usually on physical toughness or how well you can get your body to move and play the game. However, kids who want to succeed in their chosen sports must also know about mental toughness.

Losing or other bad things can get in the way of what you want, but when you have mental toughness, you know to keep going even when it gets hard. In other words, mental toughness helps you deal with obstacles. It's easy to give up when you miss a goal, or you can't seem to learn a new skill in practice. Sticking with it and following your heart takes strength.

CHARACTERISTICS OF A CHAMPION

You may be wondering if you have a champion mindset. Look at the different characteristics of a champion and see if you have similar characteristics or if you could use some practice in these areas. All kids can benefit from improving in some way.

HAVING BIG DREAMS

Champions aren't afraid to dream big. They like to push themselves to expect more. They can see themselves doing great things, even when other people don't believe they can do it. Dreaming big is a must for anyone who wants to be more successful in athletics.

It's good to use your imagination. When you use your imagination, you are more inspired to do big things. Kids who use their imaginations are open to different possibilities. Kids who don't use their imaginations are more likely to settle for less.

Dreaming big doesn't mean you get everything you want, but it does mean that you give yourself a chance to imagine what's possible.

BELIEVING IN YOURSELF

A champion knows they can do it. Champions aren't arrogant, but they are confident in their abilities. They know that no matter what happens, they can get through that situation and come out of it even better. Kids are often quite confident, but as you get older, being confident might get harder.

It can be hard to believe in yourself. You may compare yourself to others and think that you aren't good enough. Kids with a champion mindset don't let what others have to say get them down.

If you struggle to believe in yourself, remember your good qualities and all the skills that allow you to do better in your sport.

REMAINING COMMITTED

Champions know what they want, and they don't stop until they get it. Kids with a champion mindset know they have to commit themselves fully to whatever they're doing.

When things aren't going the way you want, it's easy to think that maybe you should try something else. Champions make it their mission to keep working even when things are going wrong.

Remaining committed doesn't mean you won't ever have your doubts. Instead, it's about learning to work through those doubts. In the process, you become more dedicated.

STAYING CALM

If you've ever lost a game that you really wanted to win, you know how hard it can be to stay calm. The good news is that athletes can learn to stay calmer when dealing with challenging moments.

You may get angry or anxious when you're playing sports. There's nothing wrong with feeling this way. It's normal to have negative emotions. However, you want to learn to handle those emotions before they get out of control.

While you can't always choose how you feel, you do get to choose how you react, and champions know to react calmly. They don't let their feelings become big explosions.

NOT BEING AFRAID OF FAILURE

When you step onto a field or a court, you may feel your heart start to beat really fast as you get nervous and think about all the ways you could mess up. It's normal to be scared of failure, but champions learn to overcome that fear.

Think about it: When you're afraid, you can't focus on the task at hand. Some people are so afraid of failing that they don't even try. Parents and coaches often accidentally add to this fear by pushing you too hard to do your best.

There's always a chance that you'll fail, but champions see failure as a chance to learn from their mistakes. By paying attention to what you did wrong, you can figure out how to do things differently the next time.

BEING DECISIVE

Champions know what they're going to do, and they commit to that decision. You may not know which sport you want to play, or you may not know whether you should take a shot or pass the ball. These types of decisions aren't always easy, but champions make a decision and stick with it.

If you never make a firm decision, you won't be able to give your sport your full attention. You are more likely to mess up when you aren't decisive. To be more decisive, you have to remind yourself that you're doing what you think is best in the moment.

LISTENING TO COACHES

You have to be willing to take feedback from your coaches or instructors in your sport. If you don't listen, you won't be able to get any better. Paying attention to what coaches say is one of the best ways to become a champion.

When a coach gives feedback, it can be hurtful if they're telling you that you're doing something wrong. However, coaches are usually trying to give you constructive criticism, which includes comments that explain what you need to work on. These comments are meant to help you, not hurt you.

Coaches and even older players have been through a lot more than you have, so by listening, you can learn a lot of important lessons. You can also copy what they're doing to be champions.

CONSISTENTLY PRACTICING

You've probably already heard that "practice makes perfect." Practice really is one of the most important things that kids with a champion mindset should do. You can't expect to just wake up one day and be a superstar.

Practicing consistently means that you don't have long periods between practices. Often, champions will practice most days of the week, and while you may not have official practices that often, you can practice at home by doing exercises for just a short time each day.

Consistent practice keeps you in shape and allows you to build skills faster. If you aren't consistent, you may not make much progress, and you may even lose some of your skills. That's why practice is so important for all aspiring champions.

WANTING TO LEARN

Champions don't focus on winning. Yeah, winning is fun, but true champions want to learn more than anything. This type of learning isn't like the learning you do at school. It requires you to practice and learn more about your chosen activity.

As you learn more, you can do better. You can adapt to challenges you don't expect and handle issues more easily because you've learned the basics.

You want to constantly look for new knowledge. Don't be afraid to ask questions. It's good to understand what you should do, but you also want to know why. Being curious helps you be a better athlete.

REFUSING TO QUIT

If you quit at something, you can't make progress. That means that when you start something, it's good to see it through. Give an activity some time before you decide it's not for you.

It's okay to stop doing an activity if it doesn't make you happy. If you aren't excited about something, it's better to find something that gets you excited. However, you don't want to quit something that you really love because you don't think you're good at it or it's too hard.

What athletes do isn't easy. It's the challenge that makes athletes so cool, so if you want to be a champion, you have to refuse to quit and accept that good things in life are often hard.

EXAMPLES OF YOUNG ATHLETES WITH A CHAMPION MINDSET

Lots of young athletes have been successful by having a champion mindset. These athletes have worked hard at a young age to show that kids have what it takes to be successful in athletics. It helps to look up to a young athlete who inspires you.

DIMITRIOS LOUNDRAS

Dimitrios Loundras shows that kids have used a champion mindset to be successful all throughout history. He competed in the 1896 Summer Olympics as a gymnast when he was only 10 years old! Most kids can only dream of competing in the world's best-known sporting competition at such a young age.

Loundras trained under strict coaches. He had to have a champion mindset to win a bronze medal for his team and perfect his performance on the parallel bars.

SKY BROWN

At only 13 years old, Sky Brown became Great Britain's youngest Olympic medal winner when she won a bronze medal for skateboarding. She continues to be a leader in skateboarding while trying to land new tricks that other female skaters have never accomplished before.

TARA LIPINSKI

Tara Lipinski was only 15 years old when she won a gold Olympic medal in figure skating for the United States. To become a serious athlete, she had to push herself to try things that no one else was doing.

MOMIJI NISHIYA

Momiji Nishiya is another skateboarder who has done big things at a young age. She won a gold medal for Japan at the age of 13. She encourages other girls to learn how to skate and shows that kids can do amazing things.

She's also helping to make skating more popular. While Nishiya has had to practice a lot, she also knows how to have fun.

TOM DALEY

Tom Daley is an athlete from the United Kingdom who competed in the Olympics when he was 14 years old. While he didn't win any medals at that young age, he didn't give up.

He had to deal with bullying at school and other obstacles, but he didn't lose his focus. He kept practicing and working on his mindset to eventually win multiple medals in diving in the 2012, 2016, and 2020 Olympics.

FREDDY ADU

Freddy Adu is one of the youngest athletes in history to have played professional soccer. He was born in Ghana, but he moved to the United States when he was young. In America, he worked to become a better soccer player. At 14, he joined the professional team D.C. United. It was hard being so young on a team with older players, so he had to prove himself.

KATIE GRIMES

At 15 years old, Katie Grimes made it to the 2020 U.S. Olympic Swim Team. She didn't win a medal at the time and came in fourth place, but she hasn't let that experience stop her. In 2022, she won two World Championship silver medals, and she was the first individual to qualify for the Paris Olympic Games in 2024. Despite these wins, she continues to push herself to be better and improve her skills. She understands that success is more about your mindset than being the best.

KIM YUN-MI

Kim Yun-Mi is a South Korean speed skater who won a gold medal in the 1994 Olympics at the age of 13. She won again four years later, showing that her continued work paid off. She wanted to keep competing, but she injured herself. When you have a champion mindset, you know that losses happen. Losses feel bad, but they aren't the end of the world.

NORMAN WHITESIDE

Norman Whiteside is a soccer player from Northern Ireland. He became a professional player when he was 17 years old. He had to practice with other players who were sometimes twice his age, but by trying to keep up with other players, he learned how to be even better than before. He didn't let fear hold him back from reaching his dreams.

DOMINIQUE MOCEANU

Dominique Moceanu is a former United States gymnast who competed when she was 14 years old. She had huge talent, but she injured herself and couldn't participate in the individual gymnastics competition at the Olympics. However, because of her mindset, she still helped her team win a gold medal.

ANDREW BYNUM

Andrew Bynum began his career as a basketball player just after he turned 18. He became the youngest player to play in an NBA game. To get to that point, he spent hours practicing in high school to get the attention of the NBA teams.

BEP GUIDOLIN

Canadian Bep Guidolin became the youngest player in the NHL at only 16 years old. He was naturally talented, but he also had to practice and push his body to its limit. He later became a coach to teach young athletes how to harness a champion mindset and play better hockey.

JOE NUXHALL

Joe Nuxhall was the youngest player to ever play in an MLB baseball game. He was only 15 when he was called in to play a single game. Things weren't easy for him, but he didn't give up. Rather than quitting baseball, he continued to fight and eventually made it back into the game eight years later!

MARJORIE GESTRING

Marjorie Gestring won an Olympic diving medal when she was only 13. She became an example of how practice can lead to success. She dealt with a lot of pressure to succeed, but she never forgot her passion, which allowed her to continue competing for many years after her first Olympic appearance in 1936.

[2]
SETTING GOALS & STAYING FOCUSED

Goals are something to work toward. Goals can include things like what you want to do when you grow up or how much money you want to save for a toy. For kids who want to be good at athletics, goals are important because they keep you on track and help you remember what you're working for. Goals are super important for any kid; when you have a goal, you're more likely to succeed.

THE POWER OF GOAL SETTING

There are lots of good things that come with having goals. Many kids don't realize how huge of a difference goals can make.

PROVIDING MOTIVATION

Goals make you more motivated and help you pay attention. Motivation keeps you working hard and allows you to push yourself even when the going gets tough.

You'll know that you're motivated when you get really excited to practice your sport. You won't quit when you do something wrong; instead, you'll take that as a challenge to practice until you get better.

GIVING YOU A MAP

Think of goal setting as a map. Maps help you get where you want to go, and they show you where different places are in relation to others. The same is true of goals. Goals show you where you want to go with your athletics. They also show you different ways to get there.

By having goals, you are never lost. You always know what options you have to reach your dreams. For example, if you want to be good at basketball, you'll likely want to join a team or a league. Sure, you can practice on your own, but if you really want to play, you have to work with a team.

PROMOTING FOCUS

Without goals, you can get easily distracted by other things (more on that later). You end up not paying attention when you should and not giving your activity your all. Most important, when you lose focus, your skills will suffer. That's why you need to stay focused.

Goals help with focus because they give you a clear idea of what you should be doing. It's a lot different to ride your bike when you have a place you want to go versus just riding around. Both can be fun, but if you're just riding for fun, you may never get to a destination.

IMPROVING YOUR MOOD

Did you know that having goals can actually improve your mood? Scientists have learned that people who have goals feel better about their situations. They are more empowered, meaning they feel like they can succeed and handle any challenges.

When you have goals, you become more driven. You still have a lot of fun, but you also have big hopes for a brighter future. That's enough to make anyone a lot happier.

REMINDING YOU OF WHAT YOU WANT

When things get hard, it's normal to get discouraged. It can make you feel like asking, "What's the point?" A goal helps you remember why you should keep going even when it feels useless to do so.

As your coach makes you run back and forth or do tiring drills, you can remind yourself of your goals to remember why you're pushing yourself. You'll learn that the hard tasks are definitely worth doing.

SETTING SMART GOALS

Setting goals is hard for many kids. You might not have a great idea of what you want in the future. It's normal for kids to live in the moment and focus on what's going on now. That's actually a good thing, but you also need to think about what you want in the future so that you can take steps to get there.

A common type of goal is a SMART goal, which was first used by George T. Doran in 1981. SMART stands for *specific, measurable, attainable, relevant,* and *timely.*

SPECIFIC

You want your goals to be specific. That means you should be able to describe your goal. Wanting to be better at soccer is a good starting point, but it isn't specific enough. It doesn't give a clear idea of what you want to accomplish. As a result, it may be hard to stick to the goal because it doesn't go into enough detail.

A more specific goal would be something like, "I want to score more goals during the next soccer season." You can then build on that goal and add additional information.

MEASURABLE

You want to treat a goal a little like a science experiment. Goals should be something you can measure so that you know when you're close to reaching them. Most measurable goals will use a number, but if you have other ways to measure your goal, that's okay too.

Let's go back to the soccer example. You can take the number of goals you scored last season and then try to get more than that number. That way, you'll know whether you've reached your goal by the end of the season. For instance, you can look back and say, "I scored one goal last season, but this year I scored two."

ATTAINABLE

While it's good to dream big, goals have to be something you can actually reach. Having an attainable goal means choosing a goal you can accomplish with effort. For example, saying that you want to be the first gymnast on the moon isn't something you can reasonably accomplish.

When creating attainable goals, you want them to be challenging but not so challenging that you feel stressed out thinking about them. You may do better than you think, but it's better to start with a goal you can reach rather than aiming too high.

RELEVANT

A relevant goal is one that matters to you. Certain goals may be ones you can achieve, but if they aren't important to you, you aren't likely to go after them. Plus, you won't feel as satisfied even if you do achieve them.

When making athletic goals, you want to focus on your sport or activity. Saying, "I want to be a good singer," isn't a bad thing, but that goal should be separate from your athletic goals.

TIMELY

Timely goals are goals you can accomplish within a certain period. For kids, these time periods are often shorter and usually fall anywhere from a week to several months away. You can have long-term goals if you're really committed, but it's better to start with short-term goals and build up from there.

Make sure you give yourself enough time to complete a goal. You won't be able to create a drastic change overnight, and setting too strict of a goal will only discourage you.

STAYING FOCUSED ON YOUR GOALS

When there are TV shows to watch or games to play, staying focused on your goals may not feel all that thrilling. Some goals may seem really cool when you think about them, but they're a lot harder when you actually try to do them. Staying focused on goals is hard. That's true for adults, too! Luckily, there are ways you can improve your focus on your goals.

WRITE THEM DOWN

People who write their goals down are more likely to reach them. Handwriting a goal helps you commit that goal to your mind. If you don't write down your goal, it's easier to forget it or delay taking steps to reach it. If you really want to commit your goal to memory, try writing it down each morning shortly after you wake up.

ASK YOUR PARENTS FOR HELP

Getting your parents involved is a good way to get support for your goals. Your parents can help and encourage you when you stray from your goals. You may be able to create a reward system with them, such as a week free of chores or some of your favorite candy when you reach your goal.

SET GOALS WITH FRIENDS

Try setting a goal that you can complete with your friends. Working toward a goal at the same time as your friends is a good way to encourage one another. It's a lot more fun to complete a goal when you're doing it as a group. Plus, your friends can help you get back on track if you get distracted.

CHANGE GOALS

If a goal isn't working for you, you may want to switch it up. Sometimes, you make a goal and then realize that it doesn't actually match what you want. You don't have to change goals without a good reason, but if you're too pressured or unhappy, it's okay to decide you want something else.

SET SMALLER GOALS

Lots of kids dream big and end up making huge goals. You may set a goal of being a professional athlete when you grow up. That's a great goal, but you need smaller goals too.

You want to create goals that you can reach soon. These smaller goals are like building blocks. Eventually, they take shape into that bigger goal. You won't wake up tomorrow as Michael Jordan, but you can make a goal to master your dribbling skills.

OVERCOMING DISTRACTIONS

We've already talked about the importance of focus. One of the biggest reasons kids lose focus is distractions. Distractions feel really good in the moment, but they don't have lasting impacts on your well-being. By learning to avoid these distractions, you can spend more time improving yourself and doing things that excite you more.

PUT DOWN DEVICES

Who doesn't love to spend some time on an electronic device? These devices are a lot of fun, but when you spend too much time on them, you may get distracted and forget about your goals. By putting down your devices for just a little while, you can reach your goals faster.

FOCUS ON ONE THING AT A TIME

You don't want to get distracted because you have too many goals. It's good to pick just one thing you want to do. You can add other goals as you get used to checking things off your list. When you're working on something, give it your full attention. It's better to spend less time focused on an activity than being distracted the entire time.

DON'T PRACTICE TOO LONG

You may want fast results, but you need to have balance. If you push yourself too hard, you're likely to experience something called burnout. Burnout is when you become tired from working yourself too hard. Burnout can make it take longer to reach your goals. You may even quit altogether.

KNOW WHAT DISTRACTS YOU

Pay attention to the things that distract you. When you know your weaknesses, you can keep those distractions away while you're trying to work on your goals. For example, while it may be fun to play with your dog, don't let that get in the way of your practice.

MAKE TASKS INTO GAMES

Reaching goals doesn't have to be boring. Imagining you're playing a game helps make anything seem a little more exciting. Keep trying to win against yourself and be better than you were before. Getting stuff done can be tons of fun!

[3]
DEVELOPING MENTAL TOUGHNESS

If you want to do well in sports, you usually have to think about your physical abilities. How fast are you? What skills do you have? Is your endurance strong? These sorts of questions are all helpful when trying to improve at athletics, but you also have to think about your mental toughness. Champions know that their minds are their secret weapon in any sport or activity.

HOW TO BUILD MENTAL TOUGHNESS

There are some qualities you need to have if you want to build mental toughness. These qualities may not be something you have now, but with practice, you can learn to develop them.

KNOWING YOUR SKILLS

When you know your skills, you know that no matter what happens, you have the skills you need to better your situation. Think about doing homework. You may not know the answer right away, but if you are good at research, you can look up information that will help you find the answers.

Everyone has unique skills, and knowing your strengths will help you when you're facing a problem. You may struggle in certain areas, but that doesn't mean you can't improve. Remember that skills aren't something you're born with; you can build them up with practice.

PULLING YOURSELF & OTHERS UP

Mentally tough people know how to pull themselves up, but they also know how to help their teammates. These types of people always know how to cheer others on and keep going after a loss. They know that one loss doesn't mean they have to keep losing.

When you feel defeated, you may not want to get back up. It can be painful to keep going. You may even doubt you like your sport at all when you don't feel good at it, but if you can pull yourself up, you can overcome those doubts and rediscover your love of the game.

HANDLING CHALLENGES LIKE A PRO

If you're mentally tough, you don't see a challenge as something bad. Mentally tough people love a challenge because it gives them a chance to use their skills. The harder the challenge, the more exciting it is for a mentally tough person.

When someone tells you that you can't accomplish a goal, use that to motivate yourself. "I can do it" should be your motto. Pros know that if they set their minds to something, they can get it done.

WORKING WITH CHANGE

Change is scary for most people, but mentally tough people know they can use change to improve. Our brains are built to fear change because, for our ancestors, any little change could be dangerous. While we don't have the same threats that earlier humans had, it's still normal for change to feel scary.

Mentally tough people know that change is a part of life. They try to think about how change can benefit them rather than focusing on all the scary parts of change. You may not feel ready for change, but it happens whether you're ready or not.

SAY NO SOMETIMES

While champions know that they can't just give up on a whim, they also know that sometimes you have to say no. For example, if someone tries to pressure you to skip practice when you know you need it, saying no shows mental toughness.

It's normal to want to please other people by saying yes, but people with mental toughness choose to stand by their values and what's important to them. There may be lots of things that your parents or other adults in your life decide for you, but there will also be things you have to decide for yourself.

TECHNIQUES TO BUILD RESILIENCE

Your brain may not be a muscle, but it's a lot like one. Just like you can do exercises to improve your muscles, you can do exercises to train your brain. One area you can train in is resilience. Resilience is your ability to recover from failures, mistakes, and other hardships.

Think of resilience like a rubber band. When you pull a rubber band out, it becomes tense and strained. When you let it go, it goes back to its original shape. When you are resilient, you're like a rubber band. If something hard happens, you can always bounce back.

HANDLING
PRESSURE & STRESS

Sometimes, it can feel like it's impossible to deal with all the things you have to do. When you're practicing for a sport, pressure, and stress can make it hard to focus or even turn a fun activity into something that feels awful. When you're stressed, you feel unable to deal with all the things you have to do. Stress and pressure aren't fun, but you can handle those feelings.

REMEMBER WHAT YOU ENJOY ABOUT SPORTS

When things are stressful, you may forget about why you love to play sports. You have to keep thinking about why sports are fun and focus on the enjoyable parts instead of stressful ones.

Sports are never going to be easy, but they should make you feel good. If they're always stressful, you may have to rethink your mindset and see if you can focus on what excites you over what stresses you out. Sports can be fun as long as you keep reminding yourself of that.

PLAY AGAINST YOURSELF, NOT OTHERS

Think about playing the game against yourself rather than against others. Try to focus on giving your best performance instead of thinking you need to be better than the other team. If you win, that's great, but it's less stressful when you focus on yourself over others.

Because sports are competitive, you can want to win so much that you put a lot of pressure on yourself. Sometimes, coaches or parents can add to that pressure. That's when you have to focus on playing as well as you can. That's all you can do!

TAKE BREAKS OFTEN

When you want to be good at something, it's normal to want to practice a lot. Practicing is usually good, but if it gets to the point where you're feeling upset, frustrated, or stressed, it may be time to take a break. Give yourself time to calm down, and you will feel better when you go back to practice.

When taking a break, drink some water or have a snack. Sit down if you need to. It may help to talk to a friend or just take some deep breaths. A few minutes of rest can make a huge difference in how you feel.

DON'T KEEP IT IN

When you're feeling stressed, it can be tempting to keep those feelings to yourself, but it's important to share what you're going through. When you share what you're feeling with others, it prevents those emotions from growing out of control. Feelings get worse when you try to ignore them rather than face them.

You can choose how you let your feelings out. Your parent or guardian is a great choice for someone to talk to. Teachers, coaches, or other trusted adults are other options. If you want to talk to someone your own age, try your friends. They can give you a lot of support.

If you don't want to talk about it, consider journaling. Simply writing down your feelings on a page or recording them on your phone can help take the pressure off.

DO SOMETHING RELAXING

When you've been feeling really stressed or you're under too much pressure, that's when you need to do something that helps you relax. You can relax in a lot of ways, such as playing games, building something, or going with your parents to the park. Whatever makes you feel calm is a great option.

When you're relaxing, try not to think about the things that are worrying you. It's better to focus on what makes you feel calm. You can deal with the stress later. After relaxing, you may realize that what you were stressing over wasn't as bad as you initially thought.

STAYING POSITIVE IN CHALLENGING SITUATIONS

It's a lot easier to be positive when things are going well. The sun is shining and everything is great until the clouds start to appear, and then the rain comes pouring down. Once the storm starts, the shift from positive to negative can come on fast, but kids with a champion mindset know how to stay positive in even the most challenging situations.

One of the best examples of an athlete who stayed positive in a challenging situation is Kerri Strug. Kerri was an American gymnast. She spent most of her childhood practicing in the gym to become a professional athlete. She gave up a lot to make her dream a reality.

Her hard work paid off, and she later became a team member at the 1996 Summer Olympics in Atlanta, Georgia. Kerri was still a teenager when she competed in the Olympics. She had reached her goal of making it to the hardest competition in her sport, but she still had to compete with athletes from around the world.

A major challenge for Kerri was the team gymnastics competition. The Americans had never won a gold medal in the event before, so there was a lot of pressure on the team to do well.

By the end of the competition, the United States team was just barely ahead. They had one event left: the vault. The vault requires gymnasts to jump on a springboard and vault in the air before landing on their feet, so it's very challenging, even for athletes who have practiced a lot. Each athlete had the chance to do their vault twice.

The United States team struggled to do well on the vaults. The first few gymnasts on the team didn't do very well, and the one who went before Kerri fell on both of her attempts. Team USA felt the gold medal slipping away. Kerri knew that it was up to her. If the team was going to win, she had to be the one to make it happen.

That's a lot of pressure for a young athlete, but Kerri went for it. She landed badly on her first vault. Even worse, she hurt her ankle and was in intense pain. The crowd was shocked, and they were sure the team would not get a medal in the event.

But Kerri wasn't ready to give up just yet. Instead, she limped back to the start of the vault and flipped through the air. To everyone's surprise, she landed perfectly. Kerri won the team its gold medal!

Even though things went wrong in the gymnastics competition, Kerri knew what she had to do, and she tried to keep a positive mindset. By doing this and believing in herself, Kerri was able to overcome her pain to help her team to a historic win. If Kerri had said, "I can't do it," her team never would have brought home the gold.

[4]
BUILDING
CONFIDENCE

Having confidence means that you believe in yourself and you know what to do. You appreciate your abilities, and you don't think too much about your weaknesses. Confidence doesn't come naturally to everyone, but you can improve your confidence no matter where you start.

If you aren't confident, you may notice that you often feel bad about yourself. You may also doubt that you are good at your favorite sport or activity. When you don't have much confidence, it's easy to believe that other people are better than you and that you won't be able to keep up. If you ever feel this way, working on your confidence can help.

THE IMPORTANCE OF SELF-CONFIDENCE IN SPORTS

If you want to do well in your sport, you need to have confidence. Confidence helps you deal with the ups and downs that naturally come with any athletic activity. Athletes who don't believe in themselves don't do as well. They also tend to have less fun playing their sports. That's why confidence is so important.

When you don't have confidence, it can be a huge distraction. You start thinking about all the things you're doing wrong rather than focusing on what you can do better. With more confidence, you can give your all to the game and set yourself up for success.

Confidence also allows you to be a better team player. Kids with confidence don't see other players as threats. If you don't feel confident, you may feel bad when someone can do something better than you. When you have confidence, you know how to work with teammates without feeling insecure. You use one another's strengths and help each other improve.

You also need confidence because it reminds you that you are strong and can achieve success. Playing a sport is about more than winning; you should enjoy the process of playing and learning how to be a better player.

WAYS TO BOOST YOUR CONFIDENCE

If you find it hard to be confident, you can take steps to improve. Practicing some of the following things each day can help. Plus, these are skills you can use for many years to come—even when you're fully grown!

STOP SAYING "I CAN'T"

One of the worst things you can do for your confidence is to say, "I can't." When you say that you can't do something, you put limits on yourself that don't allow you to improve your skills.

When you want to say, "I can't," try to replace it with something like, "I don't know how to do this right now, but I want to learn." Focus on what you can do, and you will eventually be able to do the things you thought you couldn't. You may surprise yourself with what you accomplish later.

When you say that you can do something, you are encouraging yourself to keep working to reach your goals. You feel more excited about practicing, and you'll know that, in time, you can get better.

Remember that saying "I can" doesn't always mean that you can do something right away. Instead, it means that you can try to achieve anything you set your mind to. If your coach asks you to play a certain position or reach a certain goal, say you can and then work to make it possible.

DON'T COMPARE YOURSELF TO OTHERS

It's normal to compare yourself to other players, but you shouldn't feel bad because someone is better than you at a particular skill. People are all different, which means that comparing yourself to others usually isn't fair. If someone is good at something, that doesn't mean you aren't also good at other things in your own way.

Each person brings something to the team, so focus on what you bring. Think about how you can improve and how far you've already come. For example, you might not have known all the rules when you first started your sport. Now, with more experience, you probably don't have that problem.

OTHER PEOPLE DON'T DEFINE YOUR WORTH

Just as you shouldn't compare yourself to other people, you need to know that other people don't define your worth. As humans, it's normal to want to be accepted and care what others think of us. There's nothing wrong with wanting to be liked, but it's important to know that you are worthy even if other people don't like you or are mean to you.

As a person, you are important. Even when other people doubt you, you have value. If anyone ever says something mean about you, remember that people usually say mean things because they're taking out their bad feelings on others. Think of what you love about yourself whenever someone else makes you feel bad. That way, you always remember your worth.

RECOUNTING WHAT YOU'RE PROUD OF

Being more confident means you have to change your mindset. Did you know that what you think before bed can have a lot of impact on your mental health? When you repeat something before bed, your brain remembers it better, so saying things that give you confidence before bed can make a big difference.

Think about the things that make you happy to be you and what you've done well. Every night before you go to bed, make it part of your routine to say something about yourself that you're proud of. You can choose something related to whatever sport you play, but it's also okay to choose things you're proud of in other areas too.

If you really want to see results, try making a list of five things that you're proud of. You can write these things down on a piece of paper, say them to yourself, or share them with friends or family. The point is to remind yourself of what you've already accomplished.

SELF-CONFIDENCE TAKES TIME

If you start to feel like you aren't more confident after trying the tips above, don't worry. Gaining confidence is something that takes time. Even when you generally feel confident, there may be days when you don't feel that way. That's okay.

It's normal to sometimes feel bad about yourself, but you don't want to feel bad about yourself *all* the time. The better you feel about yourself, the more energy and commitment you can dedicate to all the things you love.

DEALING WITH
SELF-DOUBT

Self-doubt is the feeling that you aren't good enough or you don't have what it takes to achieve your goals. When you have self-doubt, you constantly worry that you aren't doing enough. You think of failure a lot. You may even feel defeated before you even try something.

Many kids experience self-doubt, but it hurts your confidence if you don't take steps to fix it. That's why it's so important for kids to overcome their self-doubt. When you do, you will have a champion mindset.

NAME YOUR DOUBT

The first step to dealing with self-doubt is saying what's causing it. If you can't name your doubt, you won't know what you're dealing with. Your doubt may be focused on sports, but it can also affect other parts of your life.

What is it that makes you doubt yourself? Do you feel you aren't good enough? Do you think you can't meet your parents' expectations? Are you always compared to a sibling who does better than you? Why do you think you can't do well? By answering some of these questions, you can figure out why you have self-doubt.

TALK TO SOMEONE

Talking to someone about your self-doubt can help you understand it better. Adults can help you work through your doubts and what you can do about them. Your friends can help by listening and sharing their own experiences. It can feel lonely when you deal with doubt on your own. Thus, sharing doubt can make it easier to regain your confidence.

TREAT YOURSELF LIKE A FRIEND

When doubt starts to take over, one of the best things you can do is treat yourself like a friend. If you wouldn't talk to your best friend in a certain way, you shouldn't talk to yourself that way either. For example, you wouldn't tell your friend, "You can't hit the ball, so you'll never be good at baseball. You're the worst."

Instead, you'd try to make your friend feel good about themselves. Apply that same idea to the things you say to yourself. By changing your mindset, you'll start to think like a champion.

KNOW THAT NOTHING IS CERTAIN

Nothing in life is certain. Things change, and you won't always expect the final outcome. Doubt grows when you fear change. Focus on what you can do rather than what you don't know about the future.

CELEBRATING SMALL VICTORIES

Winning trophies and top prizes feels pretty exciting, but there's more to life than big victories. There are also many small victories, which are just as important. Allowing yourself to celebrate small victories is great for your confidence and reminds you that you're on the right track.

ANY WIN IS A WIN

If you haven't played your best game, even a win can feel like a loss. You may be mad at yourself or be stuck thinking about how you could have done better. While it's good to learn from your mistakes, take the time to celebrate the win. Any win is still a win, even if it wasn't a perfect one.

LOSSES CAN ALSO BE WINS

While no one wants to lose, a loss can still be a win. If you're playing for a small team that hardly ever wins, getting any points against the best team in the league can be a huge accomplishment. Even if you don't win the game, celebrate any time you do well.

ASK FOR HELP CELEBRATING

Your parents or guardians can help you celebrate as well. Maybe after a victory, they can take you out for ice cream or buy you a new piece of equipment you've been wanting. Talking about how you can celebrate your wins is a great way to connect with the adults in your life.

CELEBRATE WITH YOUR TEAM

Celebrating with your team or other players is a great way to mark a victory. It feels good to be with your peers, share the same excitement, and talk about everything that happened during the game or competition.

ALWAYS FIND THE BRIGIIT SIDE

No matter what happens, there's always going to be a bright side. Finding the good among the bad will help you battle self-doubt. Even when you think bad things about yourself, you can find good things to balance those negative thoughts. Succeeding in sports can require a lot of effort, but if you find goals to reach for, you can turn any dream into a reality.

ENJOY YOUR EFFORTS

Find enjoyment in all you do. You don't have to keep pushing yourself to be better all the time. Champions know that sometimes you have to stop for a moment to enjoy what you've already done.

If you don't enjoy your efforts, you'll lose your passion. Keep that passion alive so that you don't get lost on your journey toward greatness.

[5]
STAYING MOTIVATED

When you're trying to be your best, one of the most important things you can do is stay motivated. When you remember what you're working for, you're less likely to give up. It's not easy to stay motivated, but once you learn how to do it, you can take steps to maintain it no matter what happens.

FINDING YOUR MOTIVATION

When you're motivated, you are in the zone and ready to take on whatever comes your way. You have the energy and passion to improve. Without motivation, you drag your feet and don't feel like trying to get better. Let's talk about some ways to stay motivated.

KNOW YOUR "WHY"

Your "why" is whatever it is that makes you love your sport. It's the reason you want to keep practicing and get better. Your motivation will grow when you know your why because you never lose sight of what matters most to you.

Some examples of your "why" could be:

- Wanting to make it onto a certain team or league
- Trying to beat your personal record
- Hoping to play professionally
- Channeling your energy into something meaningful
- Connecting to other people through a shared interest
- Learning more about yourself and your abilities
- Challenging your body to do difficult things

Your why can be anything as long as it's something that excites you to improve at your sport.

THINK ABOUT INSIDE FORCES

Your inner thoughts and feelings can drive you to be more successful. These inside forces include your goals, ambitions, or dreams. Internal forces are powerful and long lasting because they express what's most important to you.

If things get challenging, think back to the inside forces that motivate you. When you remember those, you'll be more likely to stay motivated even if you're struggling.

THINK ABOUT OUTSIDE FORCES

Outside forces can also motivate kids to do well in activities. These forces include parents, peers, teachers, or your community. Although outside forces can be helpful, they can also put a lot of pressure on you.

If the pressure from others becomes too great, it can cause you to lose focus. When that happens, think about those inside forces that help keep you motivated.

It feels good when people cheer you on, but be careful that you don't put other people's happiness ahead of your own.

SETTING PERSONAL & TEAM GOALS

We've already talked about the importance of setting goals and how they're crucial to staying motivated. To understand this idea better, it can help to see an example of how both personal and team goals make a difference.

One of the best-known sports victories was the Chicago Bulls' record-breaking 1995–1996 season. The Bulls won 72 times and only lost 10 games, making them one of the greatest teams in all of basketball history. None of that would have been possible if the team hadn't set high expectations for itself.

Michael Jordon is probably the best-known of all the players on that team. At the end of the 1994–1995 season, when the Bulls were shut out of the Eastern Conference semifinals, Michael knew the team needed to work harder if they wanted to win. He told another player, "We're going to start working out." He set a goal right away to overcome the disappointing loss. He wanted to get his game back.

Michael worked hard and worked smart. He knew what he wanted to accomplish and targeted his efforts toward that goal. By the time the new season came around, Michael felt that the team was ready. He had something to prove, and he was going to show how his efforts paid off.

Not only did Micheal work to be better than he was the season before, but the team did too. The Bulls even had a saying: "72–10 don't mean a thing without the ring." It meant that no matter how many games they won, they wouldn't reach their goal until they won the championship and the ring that came with it.

By combining team and individual goals, the 1994–1995 Chicago Bulls were able to become that year's NBA champions. They proved that they were one of the best teams of all time. They took their loss from the season before and turned it into motivation for a big win.

STAYING MOTIVATED
THROUGH UPS & DOWNS

When things are going well, it's easy to feel motivated, but when things start to go off course, your motivation can crash. In fact, the hardest part of staying motivated is maintaining it when you're going through a rough patch.

One example of an athlete who stayed motivated through challenges is Bethany Hamilton, a Hawaiian surfer who'd been surfing since she was seven years old. She was excited about her future and full of big dreams.

However, in 2003, Bethany was bitten by a shark and lost her left arm. Most people would have given up after that, but Bethany told herself that she wasn't going to wallow in her pain. She was going to get back on her board and surf again, no matter what.

The result of this champion mindset is that she was able to get back on her board within a month, and she went on to become one of the top female surfers in the world. Bethany shows that challenges shouldn't keep you from following your dream. The path you take won't always be the one you expect, but in the end, you can get where you want to go.

When your confidence starts to fade and you feel your dream slipping away, don't let it go. Choose a champion mindset and continue to strive to meet your goal.

[6]
THE POWER OF POSITIVE THINKING

Your mindset changes how you play sports or any athletic activity. When your brain is filled with positive thoughts, it responds differently than when it's filled with negative ones. That's why if you want to be a champion, you need to start thinking positively.

HOW THOUGHTS INFLUENCE PERFORMANCE

Simone Biles has earned her place as one of the top athletes ever. In fact, she's the most decorated gymnast of all time. But her story isn't without struggle, and to get through these challenges, she had to change how she thought about performance.

Simone began her Olympic career at the 2016 Summer Olympics, where she won four medals and became a well-known figure. She was on top of the world, but she faced challenges ahead.

When Simone returned to the 2020 Olympics, she struggled to perform at her best. The pressure was getting to her, leading to her dropping out of several events. She was dealing with what gymnasts call "the twisties," which makes it hard for gymnasts to understand how their bodies are moving in the air.

After the 2020 Olympics, Simone knew that she had to take her mindset more seriously if she wanted to come back to the 2024 Olympics. She learned to try to find humor in stressful situations and turned fear into power.

She also used techniques like counting, goal setting, and visualization to stay on track. She learned to focus on the positive and what she could do rather than what she couldn't.

By changing her mindset, Simone Biles was able to come back to the 2024 Olympics and add to her medal count. She remains one of the most notable athletes in her field. Her continued success is all thanks to her dedication and positive mindset.

The lesson Simone teaches is that being negative or wasting time worrying about the unknown can affect your motivation. Instead, you want to learn to work with your brain to be a stronger player and a stronger person overall.

TECHNIQUES FOR POSITIVE THINKING

Champions know that positive thinking is the key to high performance. Fortunately, there are lots of ways to become more positive.

POSITIVITY IS LIKE A MUSCLE

Just as you can train your body's muscles through exercise, you can also train your brain to be more positive. You can do this by shutting out negative thoughts and replacing them with positive ones instead. You may not believe the positive thoughts at first, but in time, you will start to experience fewer negative thoughts.

CELEBRATE SUCCESS EVERY DAY

Every day, you should think of how you've already been successful. It doesn't have to be a huge success. It can be as simple as sticking to your practice schedule even when you're tired, and you don't feel like doing it. With this habit, you can find success in many things you do. All you have to do is look for and celebrate the small things.

SHARE YOUR POSITIVITY WITH OTHERS

Positivity isn't something you should keep to yourself. Sharing positivity with others spreads happiness. Complimenting someone or pointing out their successes can help them feel better about themselves, and you'll feel better too.

Positivity has a ripple effect, so just a little can go a long way in making your team, family, and friends feel happier.

DON'T BE TOO HARD ON YOURSELF

Kids who want to do well tend to hold themselves to super-high standards. There's nothing wrong with this, but you don't want to put too much pressure on yourself.

If something you normally like doing starts to make you unhappy, you may be putting too much pressure on yourself. When that happens, remember that you started playing the sport or activity because you enjoyed it and not because of scoring big or winning.

Yes, it's still good to want to win and work hard toward your goals, but goals aren't worthwhile if they don't make you happy. To get your joy back, try doing things like playing a game with your siblings or friends and not just playing at practice. This helps you remember the fun of the sport.

USE THE WORD *YET*

When you feel like things aren't going your way, add the word *yet*. "I haven't been able to reach my goal *yet*" is a lot more positive because it reminds you that you will be able to do that thing in time.

It's important to know that developing sports skills take practice. Champions aren't born overnight. You're still just a kid, and there are tons of things you won't be able to do yet, but that doesn't mean that those are things you'll never be able to accomplish.

Focus on working hard and developing your skills. It can seem scary to think you may not reach your goals, but when you add the word *yet*, you're giving yourself time to improve your skills. The word *yet* will also prevent you from getting so discouraged that you stop trying altogether.

USING AFFIRMATIONS & VISUALIZATION

You may not realize this, but your thoughts can change your reality. When you think positively, your brain remembers and responds better. As a result, you act in ways that reflect the positive change you want to see.

That's why using affirmations and visualization can come in handy. If you don't know what those words mean, don't worry. We'll go over all of that right now.

AFFIRMATIONS

Affirmation is a fancy word for thinking positively. When you use an affirmation like "I am a good baseball player," you trick your brain into believing it.

For example, if you want to improve your skills in your sport, you would say, "My skills are improving." Affirmations are helpful because they remind you of what you want and put you in charge of reaching your goals.

Here are some other affirmations you can use:

- I will do great in my next game.
- I am worthwhile no matter how many points I score.
- I put in the practice, and it shows.
- I'm happy to let others help me when I need it.
- My teammates know they can count on me.
- I can do whatever I need to succeed.
- My goals are within reach.
- I am proud of my efforts.
- I am capable and confident.
- I know that I have a bright future.
- When I fall, I get back up.
- I know success will come with time.
- I can count on myself and my team.
- Each challenge is a chance to do better.
- Every day, I continue to get better.
- When bad things happen, I am brave.
- I am a good sport when I lose.
- I am supported and loved by the people around me.
- I focus on my strengths instead of my weaknesses.

These are just a few affirmations you can use. You can also make up your own. Ask a friend or trusted adult for more ideas if you need them.

VISUALIZATION

Visualization means imagining what you want. Of course, it's a little more complex than that, but if you want to do well at sports, it isn't just about practicing hard. You also have to put your imagination to work.

Some athletes who use visualization include:

- World Cup soccer player Becky Sauerbrunn
- Olympic gymnasts Stephen Nedoroscik and Simone Biles
- Olympic beach volleyball duo Kerri Walsh and Misty-May Treanor
- Olympic and World Cup skier Lindsey Vonn
- Olympic swimmers Michael Phelps and Katie Ledecky

When you visualize, close your eyes and imagine what you want. If you want to win a soccer tournament, for example, you can imagine yourself playing the game and making a goal. You can also imagine how good it will feel to win.

Think about how it would feel to have the trophy in your hands and celebrate your victory. Let your imagination run wild, and add lots of details to your visualization. It's just that easy! The better you can imagine, the more likely it is that your visualization will come true.

If you don't feel ready to visualize just yet, don't worry. We'll explore this topic more in a little bit.

OVERCOMING NEGATIVE THOUGHTS

Negative thoughts make you feel worse about yourself. They also make it harder to focus on getting better because you're so focused on what's going wrong that you don't take steps to make things right.

It's normal to have negative thoughts. Everyone has them at some point. Thus, you shouldn't feel bad if you have negative thoughts, but you should try to change them. If you don't change your negative thoughts, you may become stuck and unable to improve in your sport.

DON'T OVERGENERALIZE

To overcome negative thoughts, it's important to keep them in perspective. That means that when something less than perfect happens, you don't think of it as the end of the world.

For instance, you may get a poor grade on a test. That grade may cause you to think, "That's it. I'm a terrible student." In reality, one bad grade is never going to make you a terrible student.

YOU DON'T KNOW WHAT OTHERS THINK

One thing that causes a lot of fights is assuming you know what others are thinking. Unless someone tells you what they're thinking, there's no way for you to know. It's important to remember to focus on your own thoughts, and if you wonder about what others are thinking, you should always ask them to make sure.

REMEMBER THAT BAD FEELINGS PASS

When you have negative thoughts, they can grow and feel like they'll never go away. But remember that bad feelings are never permanent. If you feel sad, mad, or otherwise upset, it's not fun, but it won't last forever. Chances are, if you wait, you will feel better.

When you have bad feelings, try to flip them around and think positively. Remind yourself that there are great things to look forward to, even if you don't feel great in the moment.

OTHER PEOPLE'S NEGATIVE THOUGHTS

You may hear people around you being really negative. This can make it even harder for you to have a positive mindset. Whether people are being negative about you or themselves, that negativity can spread and cause you to have doubts that you didn't have before.

When someone says something negative, remind yourself that other people's negative thoughts aren't always right. Instead, focus on what you believe in about yourself and the positivity you've created.

[7]
TEAMWORK & COMMUNICATION

One of the hardest parts about playing sports is that you often have to work with a team. Even in activities where you compete by yourself, you usually still train with other people, so teamwork is likely still needed. No matter what you like to play, learning how to work with other kids and even adults is an important part of being a champion.

THE IMPORTANCE OF BEING A TEAM PLAYER

When you're in a team sport, you have to be a team player. The people on your team should help you reach your goals, and you should help others reach their goals. By being a team player, you improve your game as an individual and as a group.

The story "The Lion and the Mouse" is a good example of how important it is to work as a team if you want to succeed at anything in life, especially team sports.

In the story, the lion is sleeping, and the mouse wakes him up. The lion is angry that his sleep was interrupted, and he threatens the mouse. The mouse calms the lion and convinces the lion that he's not worthwhile prey, so the lion lets the mouse live.

Later, hunters catch the lion in a net. He is stuck, unable to get out of the trap. The lion worries that he will never get out, but then the mouse comes along. The mouse chews the ropes of the net and frees the lion.

The story isn't about a sports team, but the lion and the mouse work together like a team. The lion may seem big and powerful, but the mouse ends up saving the day. The lesson here is that no matter how good you are at your sport, you can benefit from relying on your teammates and showing them kindness.

Even if there is competition with your teammates, learning to treat one another well can help you all be better athletes. You can go from feeling like enemies to using each other's strong points to your advantage and minimizing your weaknesses.

When you're a team player, you know that there's more to playing a sport than just yourself. Plus, you'll have a lot more fun.

EFFECTIVE COMMUNICATION SKILLS

If you want to have a strong team, you need to use effective communication skills. Effective communication skills mean that you can talk to other people in ways that help them understand your thoughts.

ALWAYS CHOOSE TO BE KIND

When you want to talk better to your teammates, remember to be kind. You should always try to treat people like you would want to be treated.

It's not always easy to be kind to others, but when you focus on treating others well, it helps keep everyone calmer. You don't have to be best friends with everyone, but it's good to show everyone respect.

USE *I* INSTEAD OF *YOU*

When making statements about how you feel, it's good to use *I* instead of *you*. By using sentences with *I*, you prevent people from feeling like you are attacking or blaming them.

For instance, it sounds like you're blaming your teammates if you say, "You didn't pass me the ball, and we lost." Instead, you could say, "I'm upset that you didn't pass me the ball when I had a shot." That focuses the attention on what you're feeling rather than blaming someone else.

TRY TO WALK IN OTHERS' SHOES

When you find it hard to communicate with others, try to imagine how it would feel to be them. If you had to live life in their shoes, what challenges would you face? How might their thinking be different from yours?

Each person has unique experiences, and different people might not think the way you do. It's okay to be different, but you should remember that those differences can either bring a team together or tear it apart.

LET OTHERS TALK

Much of communication is about what you say, but listening is even more important. You can say all you want, but if you don't give the other person a chance to tell their side, you'll never be able to understand them.

You'll have your chance to tell your side, but make sure that everyone gets the chance to say what they have to say. This prevents fights and hurt feelings.

IT'S OKAY TO STEP AWAY

When things are getting intense, or you aren't sure what to say to make a situation better, you can always walk away from a conversation. Sometimes, it is better to politely step aside.

If you're feeling really upset, you can even ask your coach for a few minutes to calm down. However, it often feels better to get right back into the game.

It can be tempting to stick around and argue, but arguing usually doesn't do any good. Thus, champion athletes know that, sometimes, you have to let go of a fight to find peace.

BUILDING TRUST & COOPERATION

No matter what team you're on, if you're working with other people to reach shared goals, you need to build trust and cooperation. Trust and cooperation mean that you need you rely on each other and work in harmony to benefit the entire team.

BE FRIENDS WITH TEAMMATES

One of the best ways to build trust is to become friends with your teammates. You don't have to be best friends with everyone, but being friendly, showing respect, and trying to get along with teammates creates a deeper connection.

INVITE TEAMMATES FOR A FUN ACTIVITY

A great idea for team bonding is to invite your teammates to go on a picnic or see a movie. Activities like this can bring a team together. Your coach might even be willing to help you organize a group activity so that everyone can attend.

MAKE SURE EVERYONE IS INCLUDED

When being a team player, make sure that certain teammates aren't left out. It can be easy for certain players to feel like they aren't part of a team because they aren't friends with the group. If you see someone who seems shy or looks lonely, try to make them feel welcome and supported by the team.

PRAISE YOUR TEAMMATES

Don't be afraid to let your teammates know when they do well. When you praise teammates, they become more motivated, and you improve the overall energy of the team.

However, you want to be careful about criticizing teammates when they do something wrong. Usually, it's best to let coaches handle these situations, but

if you know someone well, you may be able to give them constructive feedback without causing issues.

CHEER ON YOUR PEERS

Another way to build trust and cooperation with your team is by always cheering them on and showing them that you believe in them. Helping other people believe in themselves makes your team stronger and spreads confidence.

Cheering on your peers may not seem like a big deal, but it makes a huge difference to a person's mindset. When you support others, they will also support you. It's a win-win situation.

HANDLING CONFLICTS WITHIN THE TEAM

Even when you're a team player, fights or conflicts may occur. You may also be caught in the middle between other players who have a conflict. The good news is that while conflict doesn't feel good, you can take steps to handle it.

Conflicts are driven by how you and others are feeling. You may be angry, sad, or scared. You may also feel something more complicated like being insecure about your skills. It's normal to feel bad when you have a conflict with someone, but that's just part of being on a team.

THINK OF FEELINGS LIKE A STOPLIGHT

Feeling bad is hard, but it helps to think about feelings like a stoplight. When something bad happens, your feelings may be like a red light. Your emotions are really intense, and it's hard for you to think clearly. If you feel that upset, you probably aren't ready to problem solve yet.

Other times, your feelings may feel like a yellow light. Yellow light feelings mean that your feelings are still really intense, but you've started to calm down enough that you can begin to think about the situation more clearly.

Once you reach the green light phase, you are ready to start using skills to calm down and talk through whatever is happening.

By waiting until you are ready to speak, you can avoid making a conflict worse. Using techniques like counting or taking deep breaths can help you go from red to green faster.

TAKE DEEP BREATHS

Before you do anything else, it's good to take some deep breaths. Deep breaths help you calm down and can level your mood because they give your brain more oxygen. They also prevent you from acting out without thinking things through.

Start by breathing in to the count of four. Then, let it out to the count of four. Keep breathing like this until you start feeling a little calmer. Once you feel calmer, you can move to the next step in the process.

COUNT TO 10

Even after breathing deeply, it can be hard to speak kindly. In these cases, you should count to 10 before you speak. Doing this ensures that you've thought about the situation and you know what you want to say. It also slows down the conversation so that everyone can think before reacting.

Continue to count as needed throughout your conversation if you feel yourself starting to get more upset.

NAME THE PROBLEM

You also want to be able to name the problem. Think about why you're upset and try to figure out why the other person is upset. People often get upset at each other because of a misunderstanding. That's why naming the problem is so important.

CONSIDER YOUR OPTIONS

Before reacting too quickly, think about the different ways to handle the problem. Can you talk to the person, or would it be better if you both took a break from each other?

For example, if someone is yelling in your face and being really loud, you may want to walk away rather than risk staying and arguing.

IF YOU CAN'T SOLVE IT ON YOUR OWN

There will be some conflicts that you won't be able to handle on your own. This includes when someone else is screaming or physically threatening you. In these cases, it's best to tell a responsible adult who can act as a neutral third party and try to calm everybody down.

[8]
HUMILITY &
SPORTSMANSHIP

Humility means you aren't boastful or arrogant. People with humility know that losing is part of playing the game. Humble people are kind and respectful to everyone, including teammates, opponents, coaches, and officials.

When you have humility, you become a better player. That's why you need to learn to be a good sport, no matter what happens in a game.

UNDERSTANDING HUMILITY IN SPORTS

Babe Ruth is a great example of humility in sports. He was one of the most legendary baseball players of all time. Babe made 714 home runs and had an impressive batting average. Decades later, he remains an inspiration to baseball players, young and old, around the world. His career in sports wasn't easy, and he had to learn humility to be a champion.

Babe Ruth was born in Maryland in 1895. Growing up, his parents worked long hours, which meant that Babe and his sister often spent a lot of time alone. Even as a little kid, he would skip school, and when he did go, he'd cause trouble.

When he was seven, Babe went to St. Mary's Industrial School for Boys, a school meant for poor or troubled children who needed extra help. It was at this school that Babe would learn not only the love of baseball but also the importance of humility. He learned to appreciate the opportunity to grow as a player, even if that meant things didn't always go his way.

At the start of his career, Babe was a pitcher, so his focus was on throwing the ball rather than hitting them. But if he'd only focused on pitching, he might have missed the chance to be part of the hitting lineup, and that's what eventually put him on the path to baseball greatness.

In 1919, Babe joined the New York Yankees, and he started breaking records with his powerful hitting. In the 1920 season, he hit more home runs than most other players in the league. He continued to break records for many years. The key to this success was that he never took winning for granted. Some players with his record might have become arrogant, but Babe kept pushing himself to be better, even though he was already the best.

Babe's background didn't make it easy for him to succeed, but he never let his ego get in the way of his playing. Instead, he focused on staying grounded and doubling down on hard work. He always had a sense of humor and a strong love of the game, which helped him remain so humble.

He famously said, "Yesterday's home runs don't win today's game." What this means is that it doesn't matter how great you played yesterday; you have to keep playing well and working hard, or you will lose your edge.

Babe Ruth's story shows that no matter how well you are doing, you have to stay humble and play your game with grace. That's why Babe is known for not only being a great baseball player but also a great human being who uplifted people during the Great Depression when many in the country were unemployed, homeless, and hungry.

PRACTICING GOOD SPORTSMANSHIP

Champions know how important sportsmanship is. Someone who's a good sport respects the people, rules, and challenges of the game.

Think of sportsmanship as having good morals. Morals are attitudes that guide your behavior and lead you to treat yourself and other people with respect, compassion, and decency. Let's talk about some different ways to think about sportsmanship.

ENJOY THE ACTIVITY MORE THAN THE WIN

Focusing on the joy of playing your sport more than how many wins you get is part of sportsmanlike behavior. When you focus on the fun of an activity, you remind yourself why you're doing it.

If you find yourself getting overly competitive, you may put more pressure on yourself to win, and too much pressure makes it harder to play. Your thoughts become distracting rather than helpful.

When you find yourself too focused on the win, try to change your mindset by focusing on different senses. For example, you may want to pay attention to the smell of the grass or how your feet feel in your cleats. You may think about how good the wind feels against your skin or the heat of the sun on your face. Consider how nice it is to hear the cheers of your team or the sound of the ball going through the air.

Paying attention to these other things helps you stay grounded. Being grounded means that your focus is on the current moment and your performance instead of worries about winning or what other people are doing.

DON'T BE A SORE LOSER (OR WINNER)

One of the top rules of good sportsmanship is being a good loser or winner. Don't be rude or disrespectful to others when you lose, and don't gloat or act arrogant when you win.

Congratulate the other team when they win and respect that they're feeling upset when you win. Losses happen to everyone. When you keep that in mind, you can be kinder to yourself and others when losses happen.

ALWAYS BE FAIR TO YOURSELF & OTHERS

Everyone should be treated fairly in sports, no matter what they look like or their background. Being fair also means that you shouldn't cheat or act in ways that spoil the fun for everyone.

FIND FRIENDSHIP WITH OTHERS

Your competitors don't have to be terrible people that you hate. Being friends with your competitors is a great way to push one another to do better and learn more. There's nothing like finding someone who is just as excited about an activity as you are.

COMPETITION HELPS EVERYONE

Kids with good sportsmanship know that competition is good for every player. If someone challenges you, they are pushing you to get better. Friendly competition is one of the best things about playing sports.

If you have no real competition, you're not going to work as hard because you're already so far ahead. When you find someone who challenges you, think of it as a chance to do better.

That competitor may be on your team or another team. Whoever makes you want to do better should be seen as a friend and not an enemy. They may win sometimes, but if you push yourself, you'll win sometimes too.

RESPECTING OPPONENTS & OFFICIALS

Things can get intense in sports. Everybody wants to do well. When someone challenges your success, it can feel upsetting. It's easy to get mad at both opponents and officials when you don't agree with how they handle situations.

In some cases, officials and opponents may do unfair things. Whatever the case, it's important to always respect opponents and officials.

A WIN FOR YOUR OPPONENT ISN'T BAD

It's easy for young athletes to believe that if their opponent wins, it means they're losers. That isn't strictly true. Focus on your victories and how to turn failures into successes. It doesn't help to get upset over your opponent's victory.

Comparing yourself to your opponent is tempting, but it's usually an unfair comparison. For example, if you're playing a sport, your team may be better at defense, but another team can still win if they're good at offense. Each team has its strengths and weaknesses, so another team's skills shouldn't make you feel bad.

IT'S OKAY TO DISAGREE

Officials don't always make the call that you think is right. Even so, you have to respect that the officials are trying to do their job. In most cases, officials are trying to be as fair as possible. It's okay to politely disagree, but name-calling or insulting officials is never appropriate. Being rude will only get you and your team in more trouble.

If an official ever makes a bad call, don't let it impact your mindset. Focus on making better plays in the future. You can't change a bad call on your own. Let your coaches challenge any wrong calls while you just focus on your own game.

LEARNING FROM WINS & LOSSES

You can't win every game. No matter how talented or skilled you are, there will be times when another competitor will beat you. Maybe you're having a bad day, or you aren't yet at the level of another individual or team.

Whatever the case, remind yourself that losses happen. They aren't the end of the world, and they can actually help you get better.

YOU ARE NOT YOUR WINS OR LOSSES

Kids can sometimes feel like losers or winners based on the results of a game. You are not your losses, just as you are not your wins. The outcome of a game doesn't define you. What defines you is the effort you put into that game. If you've tried your best, you should be proud of what you've done.

If you lose a game, that doesn't mean you aren't a good player. If you win a game, that doesn't mean you're the best player, either. Wins and losses can be just a matter of luck sometimes. Of course, skill is important, but you don't always have that much control over the outcomes. That's okay.

LOSSES GIVE INFORMATION

A loss isn't a lost opportunity because you can learn from it. When you lose, you can take time to be sad or disappointed. Once you've taken the time to process the loss, start thinking about what went wrong and how you can fix it the next time.

Think about what led to your loss. Were you not playing your best? Were you tired? Was the team not communicating well? Was the other team strong in areas where you're weak? There are likely several things that caused your loss. If you know what caused it, then you also know what you need to avoid in the future.

For instance, if you're playing hockey and your skating isn't very good, you can practice skating drills to get better and make sure you don't have the same issues at the next game. The key is to make sure you're always moving forward.

DON'T JUST CELEBRATE YOUR WIN

After a win, it's normal to want to celebrate. You should take time to be happy about your win, but it's also important to learn from it. Just because you've won doesn't mean there aren't lessons to learn.

Think about what you've done well because you want to repeat those things in the future. You can work on maintaining or improving the skills that led to your win.

You should also think about what you could have done better. Were there moments when you struggled? What could have prevented you from winning? By thinking about your weaknesses, you can improve those areas. That will give you a better chance of winning again.

[9]
DEALING WITH
FAILURE & SETBACKS

Even when you're playing your best, there are going to be times when things don't go your way. Every athlete deals with failure or setbacks that make it harder for them to reach their goals. The mark of a champion is how well you bounce back from tough times. By learning how to deal with failure and setbacks, you will improve your skills and be a better athlete.

FAILURE IS PART OF SUCCESS

Failure has to be part of success because it's failure that allows people to learn and grow. If you never fail, you never push yourself to do better. When you fail, you know you have to work harder.

Great athletes aren't born great. When athletes are born, they don't know how to play. They don't even know how to walk! By trying and failing, they eventually learn all the skills they need to succeed.

FROM FAILURE TO MIRACLE WIN

An example of turning failure into success is the 1980 U.S. Olympic hockey team that won a gold medal in a match known as the "Miracle on Ice." The team's win was an unexpected victory, but it wasn't so much a miracle as it was a passionate team learning from failure to find amazing success.

Going into the 1980 Olympics in Lake Placid, New York, the Soviet team was expected to win the Olympic gold as they had for the four previous Olympics. The Soviet team was way better on paper, and the United States team simply couldn't live up to the Soviet stats. Just a week before the Olympics, the United States had a huge loss against the Soviets.

The United States team didn't let that loss (or dozens of previous losses) stop them. Instead, they learned to turn their failure into success. For example, goalkeeper Jim Craig improved his strategy to block Soviet goals. He learned to understand how the Soviet players behaved. By doing that, he limited the chances for the Soviet team to score.

The team worked for months to prepare to play against the Soviets. They studied the Soviets' strategies and weaknesses. They also analyzed their own weak points to close up skill gaps.

The American team may have been younger and less experienced, but they worked diligently to find opportunities and maximize every skill. They were well prepared because they knew that past losses would give them the information they needed to learn from their mistakes and come back stronger.

This didn't mean that winning the gold was easy. The team had to fight for their win. They also had to continuously respond to challenges. When the score became close, they couldn't give up. They couldn't focus on losing. They had to focus on overcoming loss.

FINDING YOUR OWN MIRACLE

While you may never be playing in the Olympics, you can still find your own miracle in any loss. A loss doesn't have to make you feel bad about yourself. You can tell yourself, "That loss was tough, but I'm going to do better next time." If you see every loss as a chance to improve, you'll be thinking like a champion.

The results won't be instant. You may need to fall and get back up dozens of times before you get it right, but that's all part of learning and growing. No matter how old you get, there will always be more to learn. You'll always have losses, but there will be wins too.

LEARNING FROM MISTAKES

Mistakes are painful and frustrating, but remember what we said about failure leading to success? If you can learn from your mistakes, you can improve. If you can do that, you can be a champion.

FACE YOUR FEELINGS

When you make a mistake, you may feel insecure, sad, disappointed, or any number of other emotions. There's nothing wrong with that. Even if you have negative feelings, it's okay. Your feelings are often out of your control. What you can do is decide how you respond to those feelings.

LET GO OF THE BLAME

When you make a mistake, you may want to blame yourself or others. Blame can feel like it protects you from criticism and negative feelings, but it doesn't help you move forward. It's better to let go of blame. Blame focuses on the bad when what you really need to do is focus on the good and then use that good to learn from your mistakes.

ACCEPT YOUR ROLE

Don't ignore your role in a mistake. It's important to admit when you've made a mistake. Even though you might not have made the mistakes on purpose, you still have to be responsible for your actions. You can't change them, but you can't deny them either.

APOLOGIZE IF NEEDED

If you've done something wrong, you should apologize to other people. Be sincere in your apology and express that you want to do better in the future. Everyone has to apologize at some point, so don't feel embarrassed about it.

FOCUS ON CAN, NOT CAN'T

When you make a mistake, it's easy to focus on what you can't do. "I can't play well" is something a young athlete might say. It's better to think about all the things you can do, like practice more, work harder, and communicate better with your team. Having a "yes, I can" attitude will help you turn mistakes into learning experiences.

SHOW COMPASSION

When in doubt, show compassion to yourself and others. Compassion is a big theme throughout this book. No matter what circumstance you're in, remember that people are human. They make mistakes and aren't perfect, but that doesn't mean they're bad.

You don't have to put up with people hurting you, but showing compassion can go a long way in helping you learn from your mistakes and the mistakes of others.

BOUNCING BACK FROM SETBACKS

Serena Williams, one of the best-known tennis players of all time, is known for her amazing tennis skills, but many people don't realize how many hardships she had to overcome. Serena had to have resilience and know how to push herself harder after a setback. Without it, she might not have ever reached her full potential.

From the time she was young, it wasn't easy for Serena or her sister, Venus. She began playing tennis at the age of four when she moved to Compton, California, a neighborhood known for being dangerous.

Serena and her sister trained with care, but they both had to overcome obstacles that others didn't face. Serena often had to practice on community courts that were in worse condition and more dangerous than the private courts other players used.

As a Black athlete, Serena had to face prejudice her entire career. Most of the people she played against were white, and she was often held to a higher standard than her competitors. Even when she began playing professionally at the age of 14, Serena knew she had to work harder and be better just to be taken seriously.

By 1996, Serena began to make waves at competitions. By 1999, she won her first singles title as a professional. Things were going well, but then she injured herself and was unable to play at Wimbledon, a high-stakes competition. However, she knew that she needed to be patient and allow herself to heal. By not letting her injury get her down, she was able to come back stronger than ever.

Even when Serena was at the top of her game, she still faced challenges. In 2011, she had a life-threatening health condition called a pulmonary embolism. She couldn't play tennis for months. She also had a foot injury that required surgery and physical therapy.

Some athletes would have given up, but Serena knew she wanted to accomplish more. She worked hard on getting her strength back. She focused on healing her injuries and keeping her mental state strong. She decided that she could either let her setbacks defeat her or she could use them as a chance to grow.

There were lots of times when Serena Williams could have given up, but she didn't. She kept fighting to do better with each comeback. She didn't let criticism or prejudice stop her. Serena's accomplishments have paved the way for other young people like her. She has shown that setbacks don't have to mean defeat.

STAYING MOTIVATED AFTER A LOSS

When you lose, sometimes it feels like it would be better to just quit. You may worry that you'll never reach your goals. You may feel foolish for thinking you could ever win.

Whatever your feelings after a loss, know that a loss doesn't have to get you down. The best athletes are motivated by a loss. They turn loss into energy, and they make sure they do better next time.

ACCEPT THAT MISTAKES WILL HAPPEN

Mistakes are going to happen, and it doesn't help to deny it. If you seek perfection, you're going to end up feeling bad about yourself. You will put more pressure on yourself to succeed, but you won't be able to maintain your motivation.

You're human, and you can't control what happens in every situation. All you can do is play the best you can, win or lose.

FIND STRENGTH IN YOUR TEAM

A sports team or any kind of support system can be a great source of strength. When you suffer a loss, you can come together and talk to your team about what went wrong. Coaches can help you understand your mistakes, and peers can help you practice your skills.

Losses are hard for everyone, but when you rely on one another, you can all recover and move forward for future success.

VISUALIZE OTHER OUTCOMES

Visualization is another tool you can use after a loss. Rather than dwelling on your loss, imagine a future win. Visualize what you will do to make that win a reality. Think about how great it will feel when you finally get the win you're craving. Remind yourself of the hard work you need to put in.

DON'T TAKE A LOSS PERSONALLY

Losing doesn't make you a bad person or a failure. That mindset does more harm than good. Even when you lose, you're still a good person. Believe in your worth, and you'll be able to better motivate yourself after a loss.

[10]
TIME MANAGEMENT
& DISCIPLINE

There are only so many hours in a day, so you want to use your time wisely. This is called time management. Discipline means that you do things you need to do even when they're hard or you aren't in the mood. Time management and discipline are crucial for young athletes who want to be at the top of their game.

BALANCING SPORTS, SCHOOL, & PERSONAL LIFE

Kids have a lot going on in their lives. Between sports, family, school, hobbies, and friends, there's a lot to balance. But if you want to do well in sports, you need to find a way to balance all the areas of your life.

Start by prioritizing your tasks. This means doing them in order of how important they are. Certain tasks can't wait, while others will still be there when you're ready.

Imagine you're responsible for feeding your dog dinner, and you also want to get in extra baseball practice. Feeding your dog is important because your dog needs food to live. Extra practice is good, but you have to put your dog's health first.

The same is true of schoolwork and sports. There will be times when you won't be able to focus on sports because you have a test to study for or homework to do.

Balance is all about knowing that each day, you will have to adjust to new circumstances. You may have to miss practice once or twice because of important family events. On the other hand, you may have to miss less important events so that you can practice. Your parents or guardians can help you determine what's best for you.

CREATING A PRODUCTIVE ROUTINE

Productivity means that you use your time in ways that help you reach your goals. For example, to be productive, you may choose to practice your dribbling skills rather than play a video game for hours. Productive kids are always pushing themselves to be better and make good use of their time.

The first step to being productive is knowing what's most important to you. If you had to choose any skill to improve, what would it be? Start there. You can then add other things to your schedule as time allows.

Productive kids know that having a schedule helps. Ask your parents or guardians to help you schedule a time to do the different things you want to do. You don't have to make your schedule too strict, but having an idea of what you want to do at what time will keep you on track.

When trying to be productive, remember that the goal is to work hard and work smart. It means finding ways to move forward without making yourself feel stressed or worried. Being productive may even mean doing nothing for a while.

If you start to feel stressed, give yourself a break and do something fun. After your break, you will have more energy to be productive. This idea can even help in areas other than sports. If you're struggling with a math problem, for example, you can take a five-minute break. When you come back with fresh eyes, you may notice something you didn't before and know how to solve the problem.

THE IMPORTANCE OF DISCIPLINE & TRAINING

If you're trying to be a great athlete, you have to know the value of training hard and being disciplined. Your work ethic will determine whether you will be an okay athlete or a great one.

Discipline is about staying focused on improvement and not letting yourself be distracted from your goals. When you're disciplined in your training, you reach your goals faster.

The fable "The Tortoise and the Hare" is a great illustration of the importance of discipline. No matter how talented you are, if you don't take the time to train with discipline, you won't achieve a champion mindset.

In the fable, a tortoise and a hare are racing against each other. The journeys show the two different attitudes that young athletes might have when playing sports.

The hare is at the top of his game. He's fast, and he knows it. He is proud of his natural abilities. When he has an upcoming race with the tortoise, he's certain he's going to be the winner because he is so much faster than his competitor. He even mocks the tortoise before the race, betting that he will win.

The tortoise, meanwhile, knows that he is not as fast as the hare, but he still takes the hare's challenge. He knows that he's going to have to work harder and be more disciplined than the hare if he wants to win.

As the race starts, the hare hurries ahead. He's excited because the tortoise is so far behind him. There's no way he can lose! With that mentality, he stops for a rest. He figures the tortoise won't be catching up to him anytime soon, so he doesn't see the need to hurry.

As the hare sleeps, the tortoise moves slowly and steadily. Racing doesn't come naturally to the tortoise, but no matter how tired he gets or how tempted he is to take a break, the tortoise doesn't stop.

When the hare wakes up, he realizes he's lost a lot of time, so he hurries to the finish line. But by the time he crosses it, the hare has beaten him to it.

In this fable, the hare is clearly more naturally skilled, but, in the end, his skill doesn't matter because he doesn't have the discipline to keep going. In the end, the tortoise doesn't have to be the most naturally gifted to win; all he needs is to be slow and steady.

The lesson here is that it's nice to be naturally gifted, but champions know that they need to put in the work instead of relying on their natural talents. It's more important to be like the tortoise instead of the hare.

AVOIDING BURNOUT

Burnout is something that many athletes experience at some point, and it can affect your progress in your sport. It can also be very bad for your mental health and your ability to live an overall happy life.

When you experience burnout, you feel like you can't keep up with the demands of your sport or other areas of your life. You feel overwhelmed, stressed, and worried. You may lack motivation; you may even hate having to go to practice when you loved it before.

CAUSES OF BURNOUT

There are many causes for burnout. For example, your parents, guardians, teammates, or coaches may be pressuring you to meet their high expectations. Another cause of burnout could be too many practices or games back to back. This can make you feel like you don't have time to catch your breath. Burnout can also be caused by physical strain or injuries, which take time to heal.

These are just a few examples, but burnout can also be caused by anything that makes competing, playing, or training more stressful or difficult for you.

SIGNS OF BURNOUT

Burnout is a serious condition for any young athlete. That's why it's important to watch out for the following symptoms:

- Not enjoying your sport like you used to
- Being nervous or upset when it's time to practice
- Feeling overwhelmed or anxious about your activity
- Struggling to do as well as you once did
- Feeling physical strain or fatigue
- Being more emotional or upset in general
- Not feeling as confident as usual
- Having more negative thoughts than usual
- Starting to hate your sport or things related to it

These signs suggest that you're having a hard time and you need to take steps to fix the problem before it gets worse.

WHAT TO DO ABOUT BURNOUT

If you're dealing with burnout, the first thing to do is talk with your parents or guardians. When you talk about what you're dealing with, you can make a plan that helps you cope better.

Your coach may be able to help you modify your schedule to reflect your needs. Your parents and guardians can advocate for you and give you much-needed support at home.

To deal with burnout, you may need to take a step back. This can include taking a break from certain activities and only focusing on the most necessary sports-related activities. It may also include finding other activities that are calming so that you can recharge your energy.

Even simple things like playing with your pet or listening to music can help. The goal is to find a way to relax and escape some of the stress that comes with playing sports.

Give it time, and you will feel better soon. Once your burnout is gone, you'll be back to enjoying the game.

[11]
VISUALIZATION & MENTAL IMAGERY

Training your mind is one of the most powerful things you can do to become a champion. Professional athletes know that if they don't master the mental game, they will never master the physical one, either. That's where visualization and mental imagery come in handy.

WHAT IS VISUALIZATION?

As we said before, visualization is the ability to imagine what you want, but we're going to learn a little more about it to help you get better at it. We'll also learn why it's so effective in sports.

Remember how we said that visualization is using your imagination to think about what you want? When you visualize, you know what you want, and you know how you're going to get there. You stay positive and confident, and that makes all that difference.

Visualization works because it taps into the power of your brain. Your brain is constantly working to keep your body running, but it also does a lot of the things you don't even realize. Your unconscious brain is the part of your brain that works automatically, while your conscious brain is the part that you control.

Visualization helps the two parts of your brain work together. Visualization is something you do on purpose, so it uses your conscious brain, but when you visualize, you also send messages to your unconscious brain. Even if you don't realize it, your unconscious brain will start to work toward the things you have visualized.

That may sound complicated, but the idea is that visual images stick in your brain like gum to your shoe. Visual images help you remember information more readily. That's why things like flashcards can help you study for tests, especially if they have pictures. It's also one of the reasons textbooks often have illustrations.

Even images you create in your mind have a lot of power. You remember things better, and your brain is wired to remember to work toward whatever goals you have. That's why the more vibrant the images you can create, the better.

HOW MENTAL IMAGERY IMPROVES PERFORMANCE

Creating mental images through visualization helps you improve your performance because it reminds you of what you want and where you need to go.

Imagine you have a blindfold on, and you have to go through a maze. You may be able to do so with practice, but it's a lot harder to get to the end when you can't see where you're going. Mental imagery helps you see the finish line.

Mental images help you take charge of your future. They also give you hope and motivation as you try to make big things happen in your athletic career.

TECHNIQUES FOR EFFECTIVE VISUALIZATION

Getting started with visualization is a little hard, but you can do it. By using just a few techniques, you'll be visualizing like a champion in no time! In each of these areas, vividly imagine and dare to dream big.

IMAGINE YOUR GOAL COMING TRUE

Many kids start by imagining the goal they want and what it looks like when they get there. This is a great way to begin creating a mental image.

THINK OF DIFFERENT PATHS

It can be hard to know how to reach your goals. To help, think of different paths and choices you can make. Figure out how they might help or hurt you. By imagining the options you have, you can more easily choose the clearest path to reaching your goals.

BECOME YOUR HERO

One cool way to visualize is to imagine that you are your favorite athlete. If you were that person, what would you do? How would you play? What sort of attitude would you have?

When you can imagine you are someone you look up to, you can embody their good qualities. That will make you a stronger player and remind you of how capable you really are.

CREATE A HAPPY PLACE

You may also want to create a happy place. A happy place is basically a place you imagine in your head that makes you feel safe and peaceful.

For example, if you really love the beach, you may imagine a calm beach with a gentle tide as your happy place. If you like a certain chair in your house, you might bring your favorite chair to mind as your happy place. Your happy place can be whatever you want as long as that place makes you feel calm.

Visualize your happy place whenever you're feeling stressed, burnt out, or upset. This happy place can help you when your sport is tough and keep you motivated.

VISUALIZE YOUR VICTORIES

If you're feeling down about your situation, visualize past victories. Think of times you've succeeded, and remember how good it felt when you did well. Imagine what kind of attitude you had that day and how you made that victory possible.

If you did well in the past, you can do well again in the future. That's how thinking about past victories can help you. You remember that even if you have losses, you can still be a winner.

MAKE A VISION BOARD

A vision board is basically a place to post illustrations of what you want to accomplish. It can help you organize your goals and add a physical component to your visualization.

If you're making a sports vision board, you may post pictures of athletes who inspire you or a trophy you want to win. The goal is to show all the things you want to do in your sport and the different ways to get there. For example, if you want to practice batting, you may put a drawing of a bat on your board.

IMAGINE INTERACTING WITH YOUR TEAM

The way you interact with your team has an impact on how well you do. It's helpful to imagine positive interactions with your team. Think of yourself working with your team. Remember that everyone on the team has to work together.

Imagine how strong you will be when you work in harmony with your teammates. What does your team look like when you are all on the same page? Visualize everyone being happy and at their strongest.

If you have issues with certain teammates, you can imagine how you will deal with those issues in a useful way. Think of yourself trying to be kind to teammates you don't get along with. You don't have to imagine you're friends with anyone you don't like, but you should imagine being friendly to them.

LOSING WITH DIGNITY

If losing is hard for you, visualization can help. You can think of how you would respond if you were to lose. Imagine yourself being a gracious loser. You congratulate the other players and remember that one loss doesn't mean you aren't a good player. Losing is hard for many kids to deal with, but if you prepare yourself for it by imagining your response, you can handle it better when it happens.

FACE WHAT SCARES YOU

If there are things that scare you about your sport, you can ease those fears with visualization. It's normal to be scared sometimes, like playing a certain team or having to do something that's one of your weaknesses. No matter what scares you, don't avoid it. Instead, confront it head on.

Create a mental image of what scares you, and think about how you can deal with it. The more you start to think about what scares you, the less scary it becomes. You may realize that what you were so scared of isn't even that scary at all.

If it helps, you can even imagine a big, powerful alter ego that comes out and helps you when something scares you. This sort of visualization can help you feel braver in the moment.

PRACTICE IN YOUR HEAD

Physical practice is important, but did you know that you can also practice mentally? You can imagine yourself practicing your sport, which can improve your performance.

It's pretty cool that you can put in practice time without physically having to do anything. This method is great for when you're too tired to practice anymore but still want to work on improving.

After practicing in your head, it's important to put what you imagined into action the next time you are on the court or in the field.

INCORPORATING VISUALIZATION INTO DAILY PRACTICE

For visualization to work, you should make time for it each day. This can be hard when you have a lot to do. Even so, you should try some of the following tips to make visualization into something you do on a daily basis.

MAKE TIME EACH DAY FOR VISUALIZATION

The first thing you need to do is find time for visualization and techniques that help you improve your mental imagery. You can spend as much or as little time as you want, but you should aim to visualize your goals or dreams at least once a day. Start with about five minutes, and you can add more time later if you want.

GET CREATIVE

Finding a creative outlet will help your visualization come naturally. For instance, you could try drawing or painting, writing stories, or playing an instrument. There are tons of ways to get your creative juices flowing; you just need to find something you enjoy doing.

READ BOOKS

Reading is a great way to learn to visualize. When you read, you are forced to imagine what characters and settings look like. By doing this, you actively improve the part of your brain that creates mental images. You can also try listening to audiobooks to get the same benefits.

START VISUALIZING IN OTHER AREAS

Don't limit your visualizations to just sports. You can also visualize what you want to accomplish in school, time with friends, or anything else that's important to you. When you get in the habit of visualizing other areas of your life, you will get better at visualizing when it comes to sports, too.

Once you get started, there's no limit to what you can imagine. You will start to see that your imagination isn't just fun; it's necessary to become a champion.

[12]
HANDLING PRESSURE

Sports are a lot of fun, but sometimes the pressure of sports can get to be too much. In fact, too much pressure can make an athlete go from loving their sport to hating it. If you've ever felt like this, you may consider quitting, but with a little practice, you can learn how to deal with pressure so that it doesn't interfere with your love of the sport.

RECOGNIZING SIGNS OF PRESSURE

How do you know when the pressure gets to be too much? Look out for the following signs.

YOU GET UPSET OVER LITTLE THINGS

When the pressure gets too intense, you may feel moodier than usual and get more upset over little things. You may also notice that you get annoyed at your parents or friends for little to no reason. When you are under pressure, your body and mind are tense. As a result, it's harder for you to respond in healthy ways.

FEELING DISTRACTED AT SCHOOL OR PRACTICE

Being distracted is one of the main signs that you are dealing with too much pressure. Your brain tries to distract you from the things that cause stress. For instance, you may notice that your schoolwork suffers or you can't pay attention in class. At practice, you may not feel like trying your best. You may even find yourself zoning out a lot.

NOT WANTING TO SOCIALIZE

Some kids want to be left alone when they feel like there's too much pressure. It can feel easier to isolate yourself than to confront the pressure you feel. This is especially true if you feel like your family, coaches, or peers are pressuring you about your sport. However, not wanting to socialize can also backfire and leave you without the support that family, friends, and coaches provide.

YOU HAVE A HEADACHE

Frequent headaches are a symptom of too much pressure. If you find you are starting to get more headaches than usual, especially when you're playing your sport or thinking about your sport, it may be a sign that the pressure is getting to you.

YOUR BODY ACHES

When you're under too much pressure, you may experience physical aches and pains, and you may feel more tired than usual.

YOUR STOMACH ACHES

Stomachaches can be a sign that you ate too much, but it can also mean you're under stress. When you're worried, anxious, or upset, it's normal to feel discomfort in your stomach. Have you ever heard someone say, "I have butterflies in my stomach"? Well, it can feel a lot like that when you're under too much pressure.

YOU GET SICK OFTEN

Pressure can cause you to catch more colds or other infections. That's because stress can weaken your immune system and make it harder for the body to fight off illnesses.

TECHNIQUES TO MANAGE PRESSURE

It's not easy when you feel like the weight of the world is on you, but there are tons of techniques you can use to feel calm and like your normal self again.

FOCUS ON WHAT YOU CAN DO

It's normal to want to try to control situations so that you feel more confident and have less doubt. Unfortunately, there are some things you can't control in life. There's no point in dwelling on things you can't change.

DON'T LINGER ON THE PAST

Whatever happened in the past, let it go. If you've won a lot in the past, you may feel pressure to stay at that level. If you've made mistakes, you may feel pressured not to make the same mistakes again. Don't worry so much about the past that you can't pay attention to the present. You want to do your best at this moment, and no other moment matters.

LEAN ON YOUR TEAM

If you're on a team, it's for a reason. Teams are meant to support one another. When you feel a lot of pressure, lean on your teammates for help. In return, support your teammates whenever you can.

By learning to lean on your team and letting them lean on you, you will feel better, and your team will grow stronger.

USE PRESSURE POSITIVELY

Pressure often feels like a bad thing, but a little pressure can be good. For example, if you are competing against another team and they're ahead, the pressure to catch up can motivate you.

That's why it helps to turn bad pressure into something useful. Instead of thinking, "If I don't do well, I will let my team down," you can think, "If I work my hardest, I can help my team do our best."

TURN TO TRUSTED ADULTS

If the pressure is more than you can take, you can always turn to trusted adults in your life, like your parents, guardians, or coaches. These people can help you work through what you are feeling and remind you of what's really important.

STAYING CALM UNDER PRESSURE

Staying calm under pressure isn't an easy thing to do. Even professional athletes can choke under pressure sometimes! That's why it's so important for you to be patient with yourself and remember that pressure is hard for anyone, especially for kids.

Being calm means changing your mindset and making sure you stay positive. To stay calm under pressure, you can learn to be more present as you are playing your sport. You can also use breathing exercises to keep yourself from getting worked up.

USING BREATHING EXERCISES & MINDFULNESS

Breathing and mindfulness exercises are a great way to calm yourself down when you feel like the pressure is too much for you to handle. These exercises are pretty easy to practice because they only take a few minutes to complete.

WHAT IS MINDFULNESS?

Mindfulness can seem like a complex concept, but it's actually pretty simple. Mindfulness means that you are present in the moment. When you are present, you're aware of what is happening around you and paying attention to your senses. For example, you may notice that you can smell popcorn or feel the grass under your feet.

When you aren't present, you're probably thinking about the past or worrying about the future. When you aren't mindful, the pressure can get to be too much. However, being mindful prevents this from happening. You focus on what's happening around you and not the things that are out of your control.

There are lots of ways to be mindful. For example, you can list the things you see, smell, taste, hear, or touch, or you can focus on your breathing.

HOW BREATHING EXERCISES HELP

Breathing exercises are a great way for you to be more mindful. They help you calm your body and your mind. You can then focus on playing your best and feeling your best.

When things get hard in life, your body and mind respond. They do this to try to keep you safe. A long, long time ago, humans lived very dangerous lives. They had to hunt and search for food while avoiding dangers like wild animals. You don't have those kinds of dangers in your life, but your body is still built to react in certain ways.

That's why when you're under pressure, your heart may start to race, or you may feel a surge of energy. Your body is trying to prepare you for the challenges you will face. This can be a good thing, but it can also make you feel worried and stressed. Sports often bring out these reactions more than other activities because they are so physical.

Breathing exercises help your muscles relax and slow down your heart rate so that it doesn't go too fast. By breathing in certain ways, you can actually change the way both your body and your brain are working!

FEATHER BREATHING

There are a lot of breathing exercises you can use to calm yourself down. One of these exercises is feather breathing. For this exercise, you need to have a feather. The feather doesn't have to be anything special. It can just be a regular feather from a craft store.

Feather breathing is good to help you wind down after you've had a busy or stressful day. After practice is a great time to try this out. It's also good to try when you wake up in the morning to prepare you for the day.

Here's how to do it:

1. Hold a feather in front of your face.

2. Think of how light it is and how it would drift through the air if you let it go from your hand.
3. Breathe in for four seconds while focusing on the feather, then breathe out to a count of four.
4. Watch as the feather moves from your breath. Start from the bottom of the feather and move up.

This exercise may seem silly at first, but it helps you pay attention to your breaths. By using the feather, you will mentally feel light and free.

TRIANGLE BREATHING

If you don't have a feather handy, triangle breathing is another good option to try.

1. Draw a triangle on paper or imagine one.
2. Focus on the bottom left part of the triangle and breathe in for three seconds. As you breathe in, trace from the starting point of the triangle and go up to the point.
3. Hold your breath for three seconds. As you do this, trace down the side of the triangle.
4. Finally, breathe out for three seconds and trace the final side of the triangle.

You can repeat this process until you start to feel calmer. If you don't like the triangle shape, you can choose a square, a rectangle, or any other shape with points.

[13]
HEALTHY LIFESTYLE CHOICES

If you want to be a great athlete, you need to know how to make healthy lifestyle choices. When you make healthy lifestyle choices, your body and mind are better equipped to deal with the challenges of your sport.

Many athletes choose to focus on areas like nutrition (what they eat) and hydration (drinking enough fluids). Healthy choices also include getting enough rest and finding new ways to train your body.

MAKING HEALTHY CHOICES

When you're working hard to excel at a sport, it can be easy to forget about the future. However, you also have to consider the long-term effects of whatever you're doing.

You don't just want to be a great athlete when you're young. You also want to be able to continue to move and play your sport as you get older. To do that, you have to do what's best for your body now. By learning a few healthy habits, you can take your sports dreams as far as they can go.

THE IMPORTANCE OF NUTRITION & HYDRATION

One of the most important parts of any athlete's lifestyle is how they eat and how well they hydrate. Getting the right foods and enough fluids will help you be stronger and prevent injuries.

DRINK WATER THROUGHOUT THE DAY

An easy way to make sure you're hydrated is to drink water throughout the day, ideally every hour. You should drink extra water when you are doing anything physical because your body loses a lot of water through sweat.

Always keep a water bottle with you. That way, you'll never be lacking the water you need. Juices and sports drinks can also help you stay hydrated, but they often have a lot of sugar, so try to avoid drinking them too often.

YOU NEED A VARIETY OF FOOD

The human body needs a variety of foods to sustain itself. Foods are broken down into three main groups: carbs, proteins, and fats. Each of these food types should be part of your diet.

Carbs include foods like bread, oatmeal, beans, pasta, rice, popcorn, potatoes, chips, crackers, cereals, and more. Carbs give your brain energy. Whole-grain foods are good because they take the body longer to break down and give you energy for longer.

Protein is another group. Foods high in protein include meat, dairy, soybeans, and more. Rice, pasta, beans, nuts, or bread also contain some protein. Protein is vital for muscle development and brain function.

The final group of food you need is fat. Foods with fat include oils, fatty fish (like salmon), avocados, dairy products, and nuts. People sometimes call fat bad because of weight concerns, but your body needs some fat to absorb certain vitamins and complete normal bodily functions.

MAKE YOUR PLATE COLORFUL

You probably already know how important it is to eat fruits and vegetables. There are lots of ways you can measure foods to make sure you're getting the right nutrients, but one easy way is to make sure your plate is colorful and has a variety of foods. When your plate is colorful, that's a good sign you're getting lots of different nutrients.

EAT NUTRITIOUS SNACKS

Snacks are a great way to power yourself. Your diet should include healthy snacks like nuts, fruits, veggies, yogurt, crackers, and cheese. These types of snacks add a good balance of proteins, carbs, and fats to help your body perform well.

Foods with a lot of sugar or other "junk foods" are okay once in a while, but you can't count on them for long-lasting energy. That's why it's best to have at least one snack you know will keep your energy up throughout practice and everything else you have to do during your day.

HELP PLAN & PREPARE MEALS

One way to ensure you are eating healthy is to take part in planning and preparing your meals. Ask your parents or guardians if you can help with meals. They will probably love that you want to get involved, and you can ask that they help you eat balanced meals that will help you perform at your best.

IT'S OKAY TO HAVE FUN FOOD

You don't need to cut out your favorite foods altogether. It's okay to have chips, candy, and everything else you love once in a while. Just don't forget the good foods—the ones with all the nutrients your body needs to grow and develop. Aim for a varied diet, and you should be good to go.

GETTING ENOUGH REST & RECOVERY

Participating in a sport is hard work. Your body and mind need time to recover and rest after a game or a tough workout. That's why it's important to give yourself time to rest and recover. Champions know that if they don't take care of their body, they won't be able to build the strength they need to succeed.

WHY REST & RECOVERY MATTER

Rest and recovery refer to what you do when you're not practicing or competing. The body needs to reset itself after working hard. If you don't get enough rest and recovery time, your body may break down after a while instead of growing stronger. But rest and recovery don't mean being lazy. It's all about giving yourself the downtime you need to be a better and tougher athlete.

PAY ATTENTION TO INJURIES

It's common for most athletes to injure themselves at some point. No matter how minor an injury is, you have to take time to recover. If you ignore an injury and keep playing, it could get worse. It's better to rest now rather than regret it later. Resting when you have an injury can make or break your future in your sport.

Some injuries may not need medical attention, but if you have reoccurring or intense pain, it's always a good idea to tell someone and see a medical professional. That way, you'll know what's going on. Your doctor can help you decide what you can and can't do and what steps you need to take to get back to playing at your best.

TAKE BREAKS

Every person needs to take breaks, no matter what they're doing. If you don't make time for breaks, you're going to suffer in the long term. There's a reason coaches usually schedule breaks during practices. You should schedule breaks when you're practicing on your own, as well.

You should also make sure that you aren't doing so many activities that you don't have time for any breaks in your day. It's good to be committed, but there's only so much any person can do.

You're still just a kid, which means that you need time to have fun and relax. Adults need that time, too, but as a kid, your brain is still developing. Your brain will have a harder time if you try to push through without a break.

GET YOUR SLEEP

It's not always fun to go to sleep, but sleep is just as necessary as drinking water or eating. Your body needs sleep so that it can repair itself. Kids need a lot of sleep. Many kids need 9 to 11 hours of sleep. Plan your evening to reflect the amount of sleep you need.

Research shows that kids who get enough sleep tend to do better in all areas of their lives. They perform better in sports, have a better mood, and learn easier. Sleep may seem like a waste of time, but it's one of the simplest ways to ensure you're at your best.

Some tips for getting a good night's sleep include:

- Make your room as dark as possible.

- Go to bed at the same time each night. This helps your body regulate itself.
- Keep the room cool if possible. Use a fan or air conditioner, or simply open a window.
- Try to allow two hours between exercising and bedtime. Exercise right before bed can affect your sleep.
- Turn off devices right before bed. The blue light they emit can disrupt your sleep cycle and make it harder to fall asleep.
- Keep your pet out of your room. Pets are great, but they often make it harder for people to get sound sleep.
- Use lavender-scented sheets or get a diffuser if you have trouble sleeping. Lavender is known to have calming properties.

These tips are a great starting point to help you get the sleep you need to perform your best. When you improve your sleep habits, you'll also be improving your game.

STAYING ACTIVE OUTSIDE OF SPORTS

Most sports are seasonal, so you may not be playing your sport all year round. It's important to stay active even during the off-season. Otherwise, your skills may suffer.

You can stay in shape by doing a range of physical activities. Whatever gets you moving is a good option. You can also practice skills from your sport on your own time.

Some kids choose to play another sport when it's the off-season for their primary sport. Playing another sport can give you an athletic edge and improve your stamina and work ethic.

Physical activity is an important part of human life. Even when your sport is in season, try to stay active on a daily basis. Riding your bike, swimming, or going for a walk are all great ways to keep your body and mind in good shape.

[14]
PREPARING FOR
COMPETITIONS

No matter what sport you play, chances are if you don't prepare, you won't do your best. Champions know that they have to put in special effort to prepare their minds and bodies for the competition ahead of them. They also take time after each competition to reflect on what happened and prepare for future competitions.

MENTAL & PHYSICAL PREPARATIONS

When you've got a big competition coming up, there are lots of ways to prepare. What you do beforehand will impact how you play during the game, so don't neglect mental and physical preparations.

GIVE YOURSELF EXTRA TIME TO SLEEP

Athletes often go to bed early before a game. That way, you know you'll be rested, and you won't feel tired when you're trying to play your best.

Getting to bed early also helps because it can be harder for you to fall asleep if you're nervous or excited. By going to bed early, you can take the time you need to calm down and get to sleep without worrying that you'll be tired when you wake up.

If time allows, you may also be able to take a short nap before your game, but if you choose to do this, limit your nap to 20 minutes. You also want to leave yourself enough time to wake up and feel alert before your competition.

AVOID PRACTICING EXTRA THE DAYS BEFORE

Before a competition, you may be tempted to push your body to its limits or practice more than ever. Practice is good, but you don't want to practice too much. When you push your body, it needs time to recover and rebuild. If you push yourself too much in the days before a game, you may be too exhausted to play at your best.

EAT A HEALTHY DIET

When you know you're going to be working your body hard, it's important to eat a good, balanced meal or snack before game time. Your body needs the fuel to play at its best.

Use the tips in the healthy eating chapter to make sure you're giving your body what it needs. Avoid junk food because it won't give you lasting energy, and don't eat anything too heavy because it might weigh you down. Save the big meal for after the game.

Also, make sure that you stay hydrated. Try to sip water or sports drinks throughout the day leading up to your game.

HAVE YOUR GEAR ALL PACKED

It's good to pack your gear for the competition the day before. If you wait until the last minute to get everything ready, you may forget the things you need. You'll feel calmer when you don't have to rush around packing.

MAKE SURE TO STRETCH OR WARM UP

For most sports, it's important to stretch or warm up before your game. Often, your coach may lead these exercises, but you may also want to do some on your own to get yourself ready to go.

When you don't stretch or warm up, you risk being injured. It's really important to start moving your body slowly and ease into physical activity.

Try to stay warmed up until the game begins. Delays or other issues can lead to your body cooling down. Pay attention to how your body feels. If it's been a while since you warmed up, do some additional exercise to get your body ready again.

LIMIT DISTRACTIONS

Limit any distractions right before your game. Make sure you aren't thinking about anything else, like your homework or what you're going to do with your friends next week. Stay mentally present and think about the game ahead. You can think about everything else later.

USE SKILLS YOU'VE LEARNED

You've already learned many skills that you can use to mentally and physically prepare for your competitions. For example, if you're feeling stressed about a game, try using breathing techniques to calm down. You can also try using visualization techniques to imagine the victory you want or how you want to play during the competition.

Remind yourself of what you can do if things don't go perfectly. When you do that, you know you can handle anything. Tell yourself that you are resilient and that you have all the skills you need to be successful.

RELAX

Stay calm. You can still be excited—excitement can fuel you— but don't let your emotions get out of control. Take some deep breaths and let go of any negative pressure you feel. Focus on your drive to do well and the goals you want to reach.

CREATING A PRE-COMPETITION ROUTINE

What you do before the game will impact how you play. That's why making a pre-competition routine can help you create healthy habits that lead to better athletic performance.

A routine gives you a clear idea of what you need to do before a game to make sure you are mentally and physically prepared. When you have a routine, you can more easily make healthy decisions. Your exact routine will depend on lots of factors such as what sport you play, your personal and family needs, and what's most important to you.

The first step to creating a routine is to consider what you want to focus on. You may want to incorporate sleep, diet, practice, and mindset habits into your routine. For instance, you may have trouble staying hydrated. If that's the case, make sure you're drinking water throughout the days before a game.

Once you know what you want to include in your routine, you can make a plan. Think of things like:

- How far ahead of the game should you start your routine?
- What order should your routine tasks take?
- What sort of behaviors and routines do your family and personal situation allow?
- How do you balance other areas of your life in your routine (such as schoolwork or chores)?
- Who can help you work through your routine?

When creating your routine, you basically want to make a schedule of what you're going to do, but you can be flexible. For example, you may say that you want to eat certain types of food the day before your game, but give yourself the option to eat them at whatever meal works best for you.

It helps to have routines with some flexibility. When routines are too strict, you may not be able to follow them if unexpected things happen, which throw you off. Routines are supposed to help you prepare, so don't turn yours into something stressful.

Also, remember that routines take time to establish. It may take several games before you really get into your routine and feel comfortable with it. Be patient and stick with your routine until it starts to feel natural to you.

Your coaches, parents, or guardians may be able to give you tips on what will work best in your routine. Getting other people involved will help you stick to your routine even when you don't feel like it.

STRATEGIES FOR STAYING FOCUSED

To be ready to play at your best, you have to be focused. If you aren't focused, there's no way you're going to respond well to the challenges you face. You may be able to get through the competition, but you won't perform at your best.

LEAVE OTHER WORRIES BEHIND

There are lots of things in life that need your attention, but when you're going to your competition, focus on the game. Don't be thinking about your homework, issues with your friends, or anything else that might get you down. Focus entirely on the game. When you do that, you will be in the zone and show yourself as the champion you are.

DON'T LET COMPETITORS GET IN YOUR HEAD

When you're facing a tough opponent, you may find yourself feeling insecure. It doesn't help to dwell too much on the other team and how good they are (or even how bad they are). Yes, it can help to understand their strengths and weaknesses, but you don't want the competitor to get in your head.

If the people playing against you say or do upsetting things, it's better to move on from those words than to let them impact your game. Remind yourself of your strengths and the skills you're going to use to play your best game.

AVOID THINKING ABOUT WHAT'S NEXT

Some young athletes tend to think about the next game as they are playing the current one. There's no need to focus on who or how you'll play next. Stay focused on the game you are currently in. You can think about the next game when the time comes.

When you start thinking about what's ahead, focus on your senses and what you see, feel, smell, touch, and hear in the present moment. When you do that, you'll feel at peace with where you are at the time.

POST-COMPETITION
REFLECTION & IMPROVEMENT

One of the big messages you've learned about being a champion is how important it is for you to look at what you've already done and find ways to improve. Even when you lose, there's a lot you can do to turn that loss into a win.

REVIEW HOW THINGS WENT

Think about the game you just played. List three things that you did well and three things that went wrong. By thinking about both what was great and what wasn't, you can have a balanced reflection of your experience.

CONSIDER YOUR MINDSET

When the game is over, think about how you felt while playing. Were you happy? Were you worried? Did everything feel overwhelming? How did your mindset impact how you played? When you can think back to what was going on, you can start to see areas to improve.

If you were feeling angry because your teammate kept messing up, you may realize that your anger caused you to play poorly. When you realize that, you can search for ways to fix the problem. You could ask your teammate to practice drills to help them improve while also learning to be more understanding of your friend.

FOCUS ON WHERE YOU CAN IMPROVE

There are always going to be things you can change to make your playing better. After the game, think about what you would want to change the most. You can then brainstorm ways to avoid the same issue in the future.

Change can feel scary, but it's also an opportunity to grow. Champions know that being open to change will take them to the next level in their sport.

SET GOALS

We've talked a ton about how important goals are for any athlete. After your competition, consider whether you want to add goals or change the ones you already have.

Post-competition is a great time to think about whether your goals are working for you. If they aren't, you may need to change them. If goals are working, think about what else you can do to stay on track.

You can also make new goals that help address any issues you may have experienced during the competition. For example, if you are weak in a certain area, you may set a goal to work on that skill in practice. That way, the next time you play, you will be better than before.

CONCLUSION

We're almost finished on our journey through this book together, but that doesn't mean your work is done. It's time to reflect on what you've learned and start using your champion mindset.

GOING OVER WHAT YOU KNOW

You've learned a lot in this book about how to be a champion. Before you can go on your way, it's important to review all the things we've talked about. That way, you don't forget any of the biggest lessons this book has to offer.

DEFINING A CHAMPION

You began your journey by learning what it means to be a champion and have a champion mindset. You discovered that champions refuse to give up when things get tough. They also refuse to let failure keep them down. They don't fear failure because they know that if they keep working, they will succeed.

SCORING THE GOAL

Kids who want to be champions also have to understand how important it is to stay focused and set goals. Life can get pretty busy, and tons of distractions might pull your mind away from being a champion. Champions know how to set SMART goals. They also know that getting rid of as many distractions as possible makes a huge difference to their success.

BEING MENTALLY TOUGH

Another tool that kids in sports need is mental toughness. Mental toughness is all about making sure your mind matches or exceeds your physical abilities. Sports stars are stars because they understand that the physical game is only one part of the equation. The mental game is another huge part of any sport because how you think impacts how you play. By being mentally tough, you become resilient and learn to handle any setback.

KNOWING YOUR GREATNESS

You also have to know your value and be confident. If you aren't confident, it will be hard for you to play your best. Self-doubt makes it a challenge to be a champion even when you have great skills. You have to know that you can do whatever you set your mind to and that wins and losses don't define your worth as a person. Don't let your negative thoughts hold you back. Take charge of your thoughts and learn to celebrate small and big victories along the way.

PROPELLING YOURSELF FORWARD

It's not easy to get out of bed and go to an early game or have to hurry to practice right after school. Sports demand a lot of kids, so it's important that you stay motivated so that you can keep moving forward. Keep reminding yourself of why you play sports and what you want to get out of them. When you do that, you will stay motivated.

STAYING POSITIVE

Champions know that they have to stay positive. It doesn't help you to think about all the bad things happening. Instead, you need to find the good in every situation. When you can find the good, you feel hopeful. You become more motivated, and your positivity spreads to everyone around you.

WORKING WITH TEAMMATES

Your teammates are great people to turn to if you want to grow and become a better player. You need to learn to work well with your teammates. If your teammates succeed, you will succeed as well. You're not the only one on the team, so be a good teammate, even when it's hard to do so. Learn to communicate instead of getting mad. Keep your energy high and share your positivity.

BEING A GOOD SPORT

You're never going to be alone as an athlete. Even if you don't play a team sport, there are going to be other players, coaches, and referees/judges around you. You have to be respectful to everyone involved and make sure that you handle losses and wins with grace. Remember to be humble when you play.

HANDLING HARDSHIPS

No matter how great you are, you're going to have hardships ahead. Athletes often have to go through a lot to be successful. Don't let obstacles get you down. Champions always want to beat hardships and prove they are stronger than any obstacle. To learn, you have to fail sometimes, so get up and keep going. Never stay down.

MAKING THE MOST OF EACH SECOND

You only have so much time in the day, which means that you have to use each second wisely. Being a better player doesn't always mean that you have to put in more time. You just have to learn to balance all your responsibilities so that you can dedicate focused time to your sport, free from any distractions.

VISUALIZING YOUR WINS

If you can imagine something, you can achieve it. Imagining what you want to do in your sport can help you bring your dreams to life. Don't underestimate the power of your mind. Your brain is designed to take information and use it to help. That means when you purposefully think of what you want, you are sending your brain good messages. Keep dreaming, kid. You'll do better when you do.

STAYING STRONG UNDER PRESSURE

When your parents, guardians, coaches, or teammates expect a lot of you, it can feel like too much pressure. Champions learn to handle that pressure by using coping skills like breathing exercises, mindfulness, and mindset shifts. Once you learn to recognize when you're starting to feel pressure, you can move forward with a clearer head.

CHOOSING HEALTHY OPTIONS

Healthy lifestyle choices aren't always the most fun. You may want to eat tons of candy or stay up late. Those decisions seem tempting, but they don't lead to your best playing. When you choose healthy options, you'll feel better and become more skilled in your sport.

STARTING COMPETITIONS RIGHT

There's a lot of pressure when it comes to competitions. Athletics are all about showing your abilities and sometimes your entire team's abilities. You need to prepare yourself for your competitions so that your body and mind are both ready for the challenges that lay ahead.

IT'S TIME TO
START WINNING

You're now ready to go out into the world and play like a champion. It's going to take some practice. You'll have to keep applying the lessons from this book if you want results.

The good news is that you'll never be alone on this journey. You can always come back to this book and review whatever sections you need. For example, if you're struggling with eating the right foods to fuel yourself, you can look back at the healthy lifestyle choices section of the book for a refresher.

Good luck, champion. You're going to do great in whatever your athletic activity is. You won't always be the best player, but you can always be the player with the best champion mindset.

Don't be afraid of what's ahead of you. Instead, you should be more excited than ever about your future. Champions know that each new day is a chance to prove your worth and become a better player.

www.ingramcontent.com/pod-product-compliance
Lightning Source LLC
Chambersburg PA
CBHW061648120626
46550CB00003B/866